*"This is a readable, insightful, funny, and wise book.
As a business owner, I appreciate the way Steve Henry
entertains me while giving me something of value.
He offers plenty of practical how-to's
on creating a winning business. Do yourself a favor:
BUY THIS BOOK."*

Chip MacGragor, President of MacGregor Literary,
rated the #1 Literary Agent in the US for 2009

THE
PLAYBOOK
FOR SMALL BUSINESSESS

STEVE HENRY

BUSINESS BOOST OF NA

Business Boost of NA
P.O. Box 22087
Albuquerque, NM 87154
www.YourBusinessBoost.com

LCCN 2010905841
ISBN-10 0-9827480-1-9
ISBN-13 978-0-9827480-1-5
Copyright information available upon request.

Cover Design: Bryan Burton
Cover Painting: Michael Gallarda "Winner Takes All" copyright 1999
Editor: Christina Miller, Mentor's Pen Editorial Services
Interior Design: J. L. Saloff
Typography: Bookman Oldstyle, Minion Pro

*All bible quotes are from the King James Bible unless otherwise noted.

v. 1.0
First Edition, 2010
Printed on acid free paper in the USA.

CONTENTS

To my darling wife Becky who had so much to do with making this dream of writing a business book a reality: please accept my apologies for my absence from our family during this assignment. You have been instrumental in providing an environment in which to produce this outcome.

To my poor mother, who suffered a life threatening surgery: you said to me as they wheeled you into the trauma center that Thursday, "He can't take me yet, not until your book is finished." Mom, I'm not sure I want to put these pages into your hands just yet. Hope you understand.

INTRODUCTION

IF YOU'RE A BUSINESS OWNER, YOU NEED AN EDGE

What would a playbook used to operate a small business that's grown over 1300 percent in ten years look like? That playbook is the manual I use to run the business I started, the $5,000 Car Store, in 2000.

Sales in that first year reached $237,000. Today, annual revenues exceed $4,000,000. I'm currently executing a regional expansion plan, having just opened my second store, with a third scheduled to open in early summer of 2010.

Did I derive my success from a savvy, entrepreneur temperament? Did I succeed because I started my business in the right place at the right time? Am I a graduate of Harvard Business School?

"No" to all these scenarios. I succeeded because I tailored my business to my customers' needs, using practical, creative techniques you can implement today to defeat your competition.

In the United States, thirty thousand businesses fail every month. One reason for this embarrassing statistic is the lack of a team-spirit relationship between management, employees, and customers. If small-business owners viewed their business model as a championship game, one loss away from elimination, the prospect of failure would look entirely different. The desire for victory breeds success. What's needed here is the *Playbook*, illustrating creatively designed plays that will lead your team to victory over its competition.

I remember my Bay Area neighbor, Oakland Raider quarterback Tom Flores, who later succeeded John Madden as the Raiders' head coach. He took his team to two Super Bowls in three years. As a boy, I spent a lot of time playing with his two sons, Mark and Scott, at their house. One night, after a great squirt-gun shoot-out in their front yard, Tom told us, "The thing that separates an average NFL quarterback from one with Super bowl MVP status is a clear vision over the entire field—a vision that leaves no room for uncertainty."

This separates him and his team from his competitors and leads them to victory. That was great wisdom, Tom.

Year after year, with only word-of-mouth advertising, I operate my car dealership with the vision that every day is a championship game with victory on the line. I implement each of my sixteen teachings in my daily life, setting multiple business records even in a beleaguered economy. I cater only to customers whom the financial world deems risky and unattractive. My connection to my customers extends to more than just a contract and a car.

My staff and I transmit genuine care, concern, and empathy with each customer contact. We do this by creatively serving their needs in a way that motivates them to share this relationship with their friends, family, and co-workers. As a result, my company has never advertised for new business. Contrary to recent publicity, Retail Trends, Inc. reports that when properly handled, this market of more than 100 million people exhibits the greatest loyalty and potential for profit in any economy.

If you are considering starting a small business or strengthening an existing one, implement my sixteen creative, inspired lessons. You'll witness how these 50-plus strategically engineered plays can produce a wildly successful business. Many small-business owners don't have time to read another "how-to" business book. *The Playbook for Small Businesses* consists of short chapters designed for quick reading.

Whatever the nature of your business, if you practice these sixteen chapters, you will see immediate results. Your employees and customers will witness remarkable spiritual connectivity leading to attitudes that attract success. This *Playbook*, created for small businesses, uses strategies of offence to combat the defensive lineup. Imagine the feeling of taking a snap from center in a championship game. WARNING! Each defensive posture has been time-tested with creative vision over a span of ten years. Your results may vary. Proceed only if you desire victory from your small business.

CHAPTER 1

PROVIDE CREATIVE LEADERSHIP

THE DEFENSIVE LINE-UP: "I need capital to grow my business, but I can't attract any banks or investors to my business plan."

OFFENSIVE STRATEGY: There's no shortage of investors seeking higher yields than those currently offered by Wall Street. Most people think they need a great idea. That helps, but the most important component of this equation is sound, creative leadership. Can you imagine expanding a subprime used-car dealership in the middle of a recession that began with the word "subprime?" Effective management attracts sound investors to a great idea.

When I attended Peter Lewis' weekend get-together in May of 2005, an old photograph inspired permanent change in my business. Through that picture, a partnership evolved between myself and another guest who shared my creative-leadership values and appreciated my methods of company expansion. That guest was Becky's brother Marc. Sometimes we can discover the answer to business expansion with the person who sits next to us at a dining table. Everyone at the table hears a great plan discussed with enthusiasm, and that can bring forth a bountiful harvest.

Dinner festivities began as we strolled onto the front lawn, where designers had constructed a canopy that would accommodate eighty dinner guests. Chefs from the Jerome Hotel stood over mesquite grills, smoking the night's entrée: fresh herb-marinated leg of lamb from their farm in New Zealand.

Wandering off by myself, I ran into Mazie, the compound's golden retriever, who would do anything for a sample of that great-smelling lamb. I accommodated her request instead with a chicken skewer I grabbed from a caterer's serving tray as she walked by.

I ambled inside the main house and down a hallway that displayed beautiful old family pictures. One caught my attention: a black-and-white, twelve-by-twelve-inch framed photo titled, "Headquarters of Progressive Insurance, 1972." This terrific impromptu snapshot caught Peter Lewis at his desk in his suburban Cleveland garage, looking out onto his snow-covered driveway and street.

Agnar Pytte, president of Case Western Reserve University, recently quoted Peter Lewis: "In everything he does, from his leadership style to how he builds his organization, he exemplifies for me many of the skills we need to see executives have in the twenty-first century."

Who is Peter Lewis? That's what I wanted to know. This billionaire reveres the Lone Ranger and named his yacht after the fictional Old West hero who fought for justice and never shot to kill. (He recently donated the yacht to serve as an oceanic explorer for a nonprofit organization..) In 1965, Lewis became Progressive's chief executive officer when he and his mother purchased a small Cleveland insurance company (resulting in one of the first leveraged buyouts) from his Father's partner. With $6 million in annual revenues, he specialized in high-risk drivers nobody else wanted to insure. Sound familiar?

By 1997, under Mr. Lewis' creative leadership, Progressive had grown to fourteen thousand employees. Annual revenues exceeded $4.8 billion, and Progressive became the fifth largest insurance company in the United States.

For the rest of the weekend, all I could do was observe this man and marvel at how down-to-earth and family oriented he was. Peter didn't have security or henchmen lurking around; instead, a beautiful younger woman followed him everywhere. He even felt comfortable enough to adjust his prosthetic leg while sitting next to me on a sidewalk one afternoon. This is the guy who was named the 366th wealthiest man in America by The Forbes 400. Known for his philanthropy, he has donated over a quarter-million dollars to the arts. He has also supported several of his political interests over the years, including Ted Kennedy, who was one of Peter's good friends.

Later that night, I met up with Marc Powell. Our relationship grew slowly until the spring of 2006 when he and I had dinner at Sadie's, an Albuquerque restaurant. The dining conversation soon shifted to the $5,000 Car Store. I pitched our business model to him, and we immediately formed a connection. I left that night knowing there would come a day when Marc and I would sit down and exchange business philosophies.

> *"...if you believe in your God-given destiny, he will make all things possible."*

In February 2008, I was contemplating ways of giving our business model greater exposure, possibly someday taking it public. Knowing this, Becky introduced Marc to the possibility of becoming an investor in the $5,000 Car Store.

Marc flew to Albuquerque in October to observe my store's day-to-day operations. This is called a "drop-in," a hands-on visit made before an investor decides whether or not to back the business. Not knowing what to expect, I prepped my staff the best I could during the week before Marc's visit. After ten minutes, he had put us at ease. Even the first customer of the morning felt the warmth of his touch when Marc took her car payment. He didn't stand around and observe; he worked along with us. The next day, he assumed

8

the role of chef as we carried out our "feed the team" concept and cooked a fantastic green-chili stew.

I had dreamed of this day but never would have imagined this would happen. My dear friends, if you believe in your God-given destiny, he will make all things possible.

After several visits to Albuquerque, Marc realized we shared the same business philosophies, and so did I. We particularly agreed on the most important one: humility.

"It's about the customers," he said, "and seeking creative ways to service their needs."

I couldn't believe it. This guy was a Harvard graduate. He could invest anywhere, into any company, but he took an interest in this small car dealership. He later confided to me that he had been searching for an opportunity like this for a long time.

Marc made his initial capital investment into the $5,000 Car Store in December 2008 and is now an equal partner in our expansion as we transform from "mom and pop" to a regional company.

CREATIVE LEADERSHIP PRINCIPLES

To succeed, your business requires a 100 percent commitment from you. Let's say the creativity aspect represents five percent of your leadership technique. If creativity is missing, the other 95 percent will not produce any fruit. Translation: "The car looks nice, but without proper fuel, it's going nowhere."

Most of us begin our businesses believing that the

principles taught on college campuses today are prudent and correct. I don't know if this is true anymore. The world is changing, and impersonality has become the standard. Call any large company and try to speak to a real person without a foreign accent. Attempt to alter an order to your specification.

When Bank of America abruptly stopped taking 941 tax deposits, they routed us to the government's on-line system. Initiating an account with them took up to fifteen business days. This impersonal action made my payment late for the first time in my business career.

We have become disconnected from personal touch, and that has resulted in less-than-desirable personal service. Here lies an opportunity for us to reconnect with the customer. I call it the "Five Percent Factor."

This is exactly what Peter Lewis realized over thirty years ago. Through a series of technological innovations favoring the minority, Peter's customers were left behind. He slowly began to restore this imbalance toward his customers.

How did he accomplish this? He began by retraining his customers to be first priority again. Once this technique takes hold, they will be reluctant to return to the status quo practiced daily by our competitors.

This, my friends, is what we must do to ensure our success. Then our competitors will be the ones left behind, failing to recognize how to play this correctly.

Here are six creative leadership principles you can apply to most types of businesses. These principles place the customer's needs first while expanding your business.

CREATE AN ENVIRONMENT
THAT BREEDS COMFORT
BY DISPLAYING AN ICE BREAKER

Progressive began collecting art in the early 1970s in order to create a more stimulating work environment for employees. Peter Lewis knew that energetic employees will produce happier customers. Their corporate collection now numbers thirty-five hundred works.

At their retail offices, they display photographs of Flo from their television commercial. Those pictures are a great ice breaker. We have our own collection on display in our showroom. It's a one-hundred-piece NASCAR ensemble, featuring all the cars that make up the circuit. Whenever children enter our lobby, they flock to those cars. Over the years, this collection has started many conversations with moms and dads about racing.

Most great relationships begin with something people share in common. We want to steer away from divisive topics such as politics, but sports is a safe topic and a great way to break the ice. It initiates fun dialogue.

What do you display that projects your interesting, exciting, and fun personality? What do you have in your office or lobby that your customers can pick up on? My dentist is a really funny guy. Every five or ten minutes, the soft music in the reception area is interrupted by the scream, moan, or struggle of a patient in distress. The first time I heard it, I sat straight up in my chair, ready to head for the door. Then I realized it was a recording. You can always identify the first-timers by their reaction. The recording is a hilarious ice breaker as you sit waiting for your name to be called.

DISCOVER INEXPENSIVE WAYS
TO PUT YOUR NAME OUT TO THE PUBLIC,
AND OFFER SOMETHING IN RETURN

We have it made. The vehicles we sell are out there in traffic every day. We put a bumper sticker on every vehicle we sell. It says, in bright red, "$5,000 Car Store." My friend Jerry places something similar that reads, "This car was serviced at Jerry's Automotive." We also give a windshield sun visor to everyone who purchases a vehicle. With over two hundred and ninety sunny days per year in New Mexico, the windshields of many parked cars read, in big, bold red letters: "$5,000 Car Store."

What can you give your customers that could serve as name recognition for your company?

SEEK PARTNERSHIP WITH SIMILAR BUSINESSES

Within your community, you can find many others who are also searching for ways to enhance their businesses. Be vigilant for concepts related to yours that might assist you in increasing your company's volume. We partnered with an insurance company around the corner and now refer most of our new policy origination business to them. Our customers receive a discount for mentioning the $5,000 Car Store. In return, when the insurance company has a total-loss claim and the customer needs another vehicle, they refer her to us.

During tax season, some of our customers inquire about purchasing a vehicle, but they need to have their taxes filed first. We refer them to the tax preparers who are practically next door to us at our Wyoming store. In return, when these nice people find out that a customer has a refund due and needs reliable transportation, they refer him to us.

Who can you cultivate a relationship with to better serve your customers?

THERE'S NOTHING LIKE BEING EARLY

If you drive around any city in the country in the middle of January, you'll see the plastering of banners at car dealerships, advertising that they are also in the business of tax preparation. Oh, and by the way, if you get them done here, you can drive off in your new vehicle. There's nothing wrong with this strategy, but I like mine better. It's got that signature of creativity. It's that "Five Percent Factor."

Most retail businesses thrive when tax refunds hit the street. Of our customers, 68 percent are single moms, and one of the few breaks they receive is Earned Income Credit or EIC. The only problem for retailers is that these refunds roll in around the middle of February. But what if you could capture this fortune early, perhaps before Christmas?

Our customers' tax refund season begins in mid-November. We purchase our inventory when it's cheaper, in September, October, and through the end of the year. In the middle of February, you'll pay eight hundred dollars more for a 2004 Chevy Cavalier at auction.

We use the deferred down payment (their estimated tax refund) to allow them to purchase in November, December, or January and pay when their refund arrives in February. They receive a much better vehicle at a better price with lower payments and loan terms. With the larger down payment, their monthly payments are reduced by up to one hundred dollars per month. This is because the customer owns a greater equity position. It also results in a much better collection effort.

This system requires an investment of capital on our part. However, when I drive the streets in late January, I take comfort in knowing that our tax refund season is over when our competitors' season is just beginning. When the consumer has his refund money in hand, he is not as reluctant to spend it as he was before he had the money.

How can you put this strategy to work in your business and capture this window of opportunity?

Our IT people have a retail outlet in which they sell refurbished computers and miscellaneous hardware. In November, December, and January, Justin now sells a complete package that includes the computer, all hardware, and one week of tutorial. He used to sell this package after Christmas at a close-out price when business was dead. He now sells early and defers the cost to the customer until her tax refund arrives in February. The demand is so great, he starts taking orders in mid-October. His sales escalated 40 percent the first year he implemented this program. The majority of his customers are also single moms who get to enjoy their new computers with their families before the holidays.

DARE TO BE DIFFERENT

When Ralph Nader, the consumer activist, interviewed Peter Lewis, Nadar asked, "Are you competing for consumer well-being?"

The question gave Peter an idea. In 1994, Progressive began publicly comparing its insurance rates against its competitors', a revolutionary move that fueled the company's growth. By placing the facts before the public, Peter exposed the truth.

In 2007, we were asked. "Do you approve most everyone for a vehicle loan?"

Our answer was "Yes!" We do this by installing a special device into our customers' cars. If a customer doesn't make his payment on time, the device locates and shuts off the vehicle. Of course, this is only after the three-day grace period, and we always offer payment arrangements before we take drastic measures.

This system allows us to look creatively at everyone who desires to own a vehicle. The result is that a significant percentage of low-income people now drive their own vehicles.

Our sales vaulted over 40 percent in 2008 because we dared to be different and tried something new. What do you have planned that will stir things up?

STAY BUSY; KEEP YOUR CUSTOMERS INTERESTED

Is your business seasonal? I've never understood why anyone would want to be dormant, especially when they have the freedom of owning their own business. The argument goes something like this: "I own an ice cream parlor," "I sell firewood," "For me, its roofing." In countless professions, the business model lies stagnant for a few months out of the year.

The ability to work is a gift God has given you. However, for a couple of months every year, your business slows to a crawl. At one of my workshops, I spent the better part of two hours expounding on the importance of this topic and its solution. I'll use someone I know to illustrate how you can overcome this with some imagination and increase rather than decrease your business during these slow times.

Daisy bought an airport fifteen-passenger transport van from me a couple of years ago and transformed it into an ice-cream truck. She and her cousin, Delilah, canvassed the city, selling ice cream to the car dealerships, construction areas, sports arenas, community parks, and teen skating parks, among other places. They sold the best homemade sherbets and ice cream I've ever tasted.

This mobile company was appropriately named "Wild Flowers" after the ladies' beauty, personalities, and first names. They did extremely well in the summer months, but when winter came, they succumbed to the conditions of their market and went dormant.

One cool day, Delilah came to my store and sat next to

me. "What can we do for the three months of downtime?" It happened to be Friday, and we served chili to our customers that day. I grabbed a bowl and ladled out a hefty portion for her. "What kind of soups do you girls serve?"

It was that easy. They developed a reputation for cream of cheddar, potato, and minestrone soups and delivered them the way they delivered ice cream. It's a huge success. Their van no longer sits idle; it runs year-round.

Successful businesses all have one thing in common: through creative leadership techniques, they enhance their customer's experience.

THE TAKEAWAY: I might have persuaded Marc to make the initial trip to Albuquerque, but it was our customers' jubilance that convinced him to stay and invest. What are your customers saying about your business? If you don't know the answer you won't be able to attract any investment talent to your company. It's that important.

The late, great head coach of the San Francisco Forty-Niners, Bill Walsh, put it best after his first Super Bowl victory: "You start by knowing that most of what you try to do will fail. A team just doesn't have a big gainer on every play. You have to be seasoned enough to withstand frustration, but when an opportunity presents itself, often without warning, you must be ready to lead. New plays just don't drop from heaven."

Or do they, Bill? They derive from a coach's knowledge of the game and an examination of all the possible approaches.

CHAPTER 2

SALARY CAPS SHOULDN'T MATTER

THE DEFENSIVE LINE-UP: "My business doesn't make enough money to pay the bills."

OFFENSIVE STRATEGY: Stop thinking that all you need is a short-term solution. Start believing you already have an internal pool of endless capital. Where is this miracle found? It's closer than you might think. The investment you make in your team's infrastructure will generate endless amounts of cash for years to come.

～

CREATING WEALTH RESPONSIBLY

This chapter explains how to use creative principles to navigate your finances so that you can create wealth responsibly. Imagine this. All your assets are secured in a blind trust with God as your trustee. No reason to worry, right? You can trust God; after all, everything belongs to him.

But can God trust you?

You need his trust in order to handle your business finances successfully. Under the umbrella of his trust, you provide extremely well for yourself and your family. However, the level of your success will be determined by how you distribute your wealth to others.

Contrary to secular thinking, we can greatly increase our wealth by distributing money to others, using basic principles. But more important, giving will first restore and improve the lives of everyone you touch.

Winston Churchill said it best: "You can work hard for the things you accumulate in life, but your life won't be judged on how much you have, rather on how you served the lives of others." If you cannot honestly walk this path, you'll become a sad statistic: a failed business.

Jesus said, "No one can serve two masters. Either he will hate the one and love the other, or he will be devoted to the one and despise the other. You cannot serve God and money," (Matthew 6:24).

The master Jesus speaks of that competes with God is money. This brings to the table a question: Can you own a small business and create wealth for yourself?

I believe it's our only hope. Unfortunately, we often confuse it with the mirage that wealth is created by the amount of money we possess. Not true.

Approximately 90 percent of American businesses are family-owned. The probability of failure within the first year is over 70 percent. In a recent Internet article, "Building Your Own Business," Steve Forbes said, "The number one reason for this demise is lack bank financing and capital" (www.forbes.com).

> *"You'll discover the answer to your capital shortfall within your personal relationships."*

I believe this is true, but it's not capital between banks and owners that's required. Rather, business owners need to adopt a Spirit-led investment approach. This begins with personal relationships first. Private investors can provide you with all the capital you need. Don't waste your time knocking at the door of a financial institution. They won't understand the complexities of your business model.

My relationship with a certain large bank was about as strong as you can have. I was turned down for a small line of credit a few years ago because of the nature of my business. ("Oh, no; it's used-car sales!")

You'll discover the answer to your capital shortfall within your personal relationships. It's up to you as a steward to distribute that capital. The principles of stewardship will lead to more fruit at harvest time than we can fathom. This concept was initiated long before capitalism was created.

The mainstream business community insists that you purchase their books, publications, and seminars so you can learn to make as much money as possible, thus warding off failure. This is the master that Jesus warned us about. These condescending attitudes, although they are the status quo, are the reason we find ourselves in our current state of affairs. It's been proven over time that throwing money at an idea or newly invented fad doesn't guarantee success. Quite the contrary.

What's needed is spirit capital generated by the people for a return to the people. This attitude originates from your heart and, if genuine, will allow you to prosper beyond anything you can imagine. Customers responding to your sincere generosity will, over time, create an infrastructure that will increase your odds of survival.

As I pore over the filings of business failures, I see that the last question on the last page is "Why did you fail?" Nine times out of ten, it's the same reason: "I ran out of capital." Aside from poor management, the root problem is that the owners didn't have that personal relationship with their most treasured asset: their customers.

Long before you thought about owning a business, God equipped you with gifted energy to help you excel in your endeavor. Next he wanted to see whether you could be accountable and trustworthy with the money he provides.

This is your test as a steward. He will dispense capital to you in small quantities. If you prove yourself responsible and trustworthy, he will give more. If you fail at these small assignments, don't expect any further financial promotions.

A test could be as simple as a company failing to charge you for an item. What will you do—notify the company and ask for a bill or keep the money? Harsh as this sounds, integrity in finances is one way you can become wealthy when owning your own business. Becoming a great steward requires doing the right thing financially, especially when no one is watching.

THE EIGHT ACTS OF STEWARDSHIP:

We use eight acts of stewardship daily at the $5,000 Car Store. Your business may not need this many. My friend Stephanie, who has a housekeeping business, uses only four in her business, but they are extremely effective.

She shared one with me that I think is awesome. Stephanie's two employees, Mercedes and Tanya, have a total of nine children and have been with her for five years. Stephanie receives Christmas bonuses from the clients whose homes she cleans herself, but instead of keeping that money, she gives 75 percent of it to Mercedes and Tanya.

This act of stewardship, obviously pleasing to him, has resulted in an increase in clients for Stephanie even as the demand for housecleaning evaporates. She acquired eight additional houses this year.

Before I pay anyone, I implement stewardship principles to enhance people's lives. The results speak for themselves. I've created more than a million dollars of wealth since I initiated these principles five years ago. And you guessed correctly: prior to this focus on stewardship, my financial statement, or lack of it, was in ruins.

THE JUAN CARLOS STORY

When Mr. Carlos purchased a red Saturn SL-1 in February of 2007, we all knew it would be a rental, not a purchase contract. (By the way, we don't rent cars.)

He had tried to purchase a vehicle at our store several times the year before. I was never sure just what prevented me from selling him a car; perhaps it was the Coors Light breath he carried around 24/7 or his lack of full-time employment. Juan was a gifted detailer, but because of his demons, his jobs didn't last. Maybe his zero down payment, or the whiskey collision dent in the front end of his car held me back.

Regardless, there was no way this man was ever going to purchase a vehicle anywhere. Here at our ministry, we try to help everyone to buy a car despite their circumstances, even Mr. Carlos. So we struck a deal with him.

Three payments later, our suspicions proved correct. We repossessed his vehicle without incident. Five months after his repo, in October, we needed to hire a detailer. At a staff meeting, I formally announced that Mr. Carlos would start the following Monday.

After everyone finished laughing, it became obvious to them that I was serious. My employees, who believe deeply in the guided principles of this book, thought that this time Steve had spent too much time in the Albuquerque sun.

Mr. Carlos just celebrated his two-year anniversary with the $5,000 Car Store. He drives a company-furnished Buick Century. Later this year, I'll start traveling outside New Mexico to purchase vehicles, and he will become my personal assistant.

Look into the hearts of those seeking renewal. They are the ones wishing to be saved. Once saved, they become real assets.

TIPPING OUR DELIVERY DRIVERS

Every time a delivery arrives, we proudly pay the driver seven dollars for his efforts. I recall that not long ago, I was the one who had to pick up those supplies.

HELPING CUSTOMERS WITH THEIR REPAIRS

We know that when we sell a vehicle, the customer probably has just enough money for gas and insurance. Again more than two-thirds of our customers are single mothers. These cars might get an oil change every six thousand miles if we're lucky.

Therefore, it is imperative that we oversee the vehicles' maintenance. When a car needs a repair, we pay for and complete the work at one of our shops. We always consider the customer's financial circumstances when we make payment arrangements so he doesn't have to pay more than he can afford. We frequently cover the costs ourselves with no charge to the customer. These after-sale repairs can total up to 7 percent of our monthly revenues.

EMPOWERING OUR EMPLOYEES

Doing business the "5K way," as we like to refer to it, is about only one thing: exceeding our customers' and employees' expectations.

We value and reward team spirit, commitment, and loyalty. After two years of service, our managers qualify for our down-payment assistance program so they can buy their own homes. Many of our employees live in my homes with below-market rents. Several drive company vehicles at reduced cost.

We also promote our employees into their own businesses. These businesses then serve the $5000 Car Store as vendors. Our paint shop and two mechanic shops began with our investment into the owners' spirit capital. Ask any football scout whether he would rather groom a seventh-grader or a high-school senior. He'll tell you, "Nurturing from within, allowing for maturity, always produces the better athlete."

When asked how we help our staff start new businesses, we confess that we reinvest some of the profit back into our people. Everyone who works for us knows that if they ever need help solving a problem, either personal or business, I am here for them. No matter what. Making a difference in the lives of others is contagious.

CASHING OUR CUSTOMERS' PAYROLL CHECKS

In New Mexico, you might pay service fees of up to five percent of your paycheck in order to cash it. To our average customer who receives a biweekly paycheck, that represents thirty-five dollars snatched away by a financial institution.

Our customers work way too hard and should not have to endure this scheme. They know that on their payday, we will gladly cash their checks at no charge.

NEVER A LATE FEE

We have never imposed a late fee onto a customer's car payment. We make payment arrangements and are always willing to help them through their rough financial times.

ASSISTING WITH DOWN PAYMENTS

Most of our customers can not afford to pay five hundred to a thousand dollars as a down payment on a vehicle. We have a special program to assist them. It costs our company approximately $150,000 a year. We can usually count on our customers to refer their family and friends to us, which helps replace the shortfall.

WE DON'T ADVERTISE

The most effective advertising I've ever seen is a customer telling one of her friends, co-workers, or family members how satisfied she is with our product or the level of service we offer.

It's true; you will never see an advertisement for the $5,000 Car Store. We continue to set multiple records, month after month, year after year, as our competitors slowly erode away, blaming lack of sufficient capital. We give a generous financial compensation every time a customer or friendly competitor sends us someone who purchases a vehicle.

We put these stewardship principles to work within our business. God has blessed my business to the extent that I have distributed the wealth back to the fabric of my network and put people first instead of focusing only on my profit. Spirit capital is far more valuable than venture capital; after all, it's people who produce the wealth in the world.

THE TAKEAWAY: These are difficult times for many business owners. Money may be tight, you may struggle at the month's end, and you may spend hours prioritizing who to pay next, not to mention the reality of checking the caller ID to make sure it's not a creditor calling.

I know that pressure. Take comfort in knowing that I remember that stress.

My answer to you is: please try this. If you're contemplating how to escape the current financial environment, then I urge you to locate an area in your business where you can act as a steward. The turnaround is swift and effective immediately.

The first time I invested money in my customers' needs, it seemed like a long shot. However, it served me well. Despite lots of advice to the contrary, I decided to take care of my customers' vehicle repairs. I scratched out "advertising" in our budget and wrote in "After-sales repairs." Used-car dealers hide behind the facade they call "as-is". I knew that if I took care of and paid for those after-sale repairs, word would spread quickly. My customers responded within two months. I receive more referrals based on this practice than on any other.

28

How can your business reach out and capture your customers' hearts? This act of stewardship will produce results that will last.

CHAPTER 3

A VISION OF VICTORY

THE DEFENSIVE LINE-UP: "I can't seem to stay focused. I'm constantly changing my mind. My business struggles because of it."

OFFENSIVE STRATEGY: You need the vision of victory. It could come from select people who enter your life, or a distinct play might be called in from above. When you gravitate in the direction toward which your vision guides you, the momentum will leave you way too busy to worry about insecurities.

〜

A SPECIAL THANK-YOU

At seventeen years of age, I was confronted with the typical decisions that faced a young man graduating from high school. However, in 1978 our community offered only four choices: joining my high school buddies in growing marijuana, fishing for salmon in the commercial fleet, cutting down redwoods for the local mill, or working in a fine dining establishment. Seeking alternatives at that time was not an option, until one Tuesday night, in the fall of 1977.

My life changed its course because one man took a few moments of his precious time to reinforce a vision.

Alan Alda

February 25, 2010

Dear Steve,

Thank you very much for your letter and all of your kind words. I am glad that in some small way, I was able to encourage you to follow your dreams.

I wish you all the best.

Sincerely,

At the age of seventeen, I proudly held the prestigious title of head chef at a premier Northern California inn, the Little River Inn. I enjoyed the work but wasn't sure whether to pursue a career in the culinary arts. With only six months left before graduation, I had to decide soon whether I'd head to Diablo Valley College's culinary school in the fall.

The sitcom, *M.A.S.H.* was ranked number one in its time slot on the CBS network. When I got home on Monday nights, the first thing I did was rewind the VHS and watch the latest episode. Not only was this my favorite show, Alan Alda (Capt. Benjamin "Hawkeye" Pierce) was my favorite actor.

When I discovered he and Ellen Burstyn were filming their new movie, *Same Time Next Year*, three miles away, I thought how cool it would be to catch a glimpse of him while they shot an outside scene. However, they stayed close to their location in the bed-and-breakfast retreat, the Heritage House. When only one week of filming remained, no one from our town had laid eyes on Alda or Burstyn.

My shift at the Little River Inn began after school at 3:30. Nothing was special about this particular Tuesday as I arrived to work and started the preparations for our 6:00 opening.

Our staff was light that evening, since Tuesday was the slowest night of the week. My prep cook, dishwasher, and I were listing to Fleetwood Mac's *Rumours* when the service door between the kitchen and dining room flew open.

"Oh, my God! They're here!" Carol, the waitress, barreled through the door.

The staff gave her that look. *Who?*

I knew who. This was the opportunity I'd been waiting for. But wait, it was only 5:00, and nothing we'd prepared was ready yet.

"I don't know what to do." Carol's wide-eyed gaze landed on me, the chef in charge. "No one was in the bar or reception area, so they walked right through to the dining room and sat down."

Duke, the night manager, finally surfaced from his alcohol-induced disappearing act. He rushed to the kitchen and informed me that Mr. Alda and Ms. Burstyn were on a forty-five-minute break from their shooting and heard about the inn's famous fresh seafood.

I couldn't have imagined anything more exciting than my favorite actor sitting in the next room, waiting for me to serve him a meal. No way was I going to let him walk out of here without eating dinner and giving me an autograph. I had to act swiftly.

Through the window, I caught my first glimpse of Alan Alda. There he was, chatting with Ms. Burstyn at table number four, a beautiful, secluded table next to a corner window that captured a spectacular view of the inn's botanical gardens.

I turned to Carol. "Tell them we're not open yet, but if they'll give me a few minutes, I'll make sure they have a great meal."

Carol took a moment to compose herself, then she drew a deep breath and darted through the swinging door to the dining room. Within minutes, she returned to the kitchen.

"They're really nice and understood that we're not open

yet. They said whatever Steve wants to prepare is fine with them, as long as it's fresh fish."

I sautéed some fresh petrale sole in a Sauvignon Blanc and garlic reduced cream sauce and served it with wild mushroom rice pilaf and a fresh autumn vegetable medley. Glancing through the window, I could see they were enjoying their meal.

The question now was how I would make my introduction. I succumbed to asking Carol to take a menu to their table and have Mr. Alda autograph it for me. Upon her return, her face already showed the news I didn't wish to hear. She told me that he didn't give autographs.

Well, that was that, or so I thought.

I turned from the swinging door and went back to seasoning the soup. I reached for the pestle, realizing that my golden opportunity was crushed like the fresh basil in my mortar.

"Steve?"

I turned around, and there stood Mr. Alan Alda. The shiver edging up my spine was so intense that my skin stung.

"I'm sorry about my 'no autograph' policy. But thanks for a spectacular meal. I'm astonished that someone so young has such terrific culinary talent." He shook my hand. "Stay the course. This vision you see is the one you must follow. You have a terrific future ahead of you in the culinary field."

Later I found out that my staff could see him, but they didn't hear a word he said. I believe this was because Mr. Alda was truly speaking to my heart.

His observation proved correct. In 1979, I graduated with

top honors as Chef of the Year from Diablo Valley College in Concord, California. I never forgot what Alan Alda told me that night. I believe my favorite actor let me know I was on the correct path. The movie, *Same Time Next Year*, debuted on November 22, 1978 in New York and was an inspiration to my vision for years to come.

How often has an encounter with someone you just met helped you to stay on course, adjust your direction, or strike out into new waters? These are Spirit-led visions. They are worth paying attention to, as we'll see shortly.

LISTEN FOR CREATIVE VISION

This chapter will show you two distinct ways to listen for those creative visions and apply them toward a winning strategy. Then you can avoid the wrong turns in life, taking the ones that ensure success instead.

God sometimes uses people to show you the right path. You can't control the blustery winds of life, but you can learn how to adjust the inner sail to tack into his provision. This will enable you to make great business decisions based on spiritual guidance and leave behind the spontaneous decisions we later regret.

What's the difference? Do you ever wonder why some people succeed and others don't? Is it the luck of the draw? No.

Successful people are those who have a clear vision of their destiny. They make fewer judgment errors, because they are able to see their path more clearly. They play to win.

Most championship-game winners clearly dominate their competitors. They have a game plan, and they execute that plan.

Those who believe in creative competition have a clear advantage when they use the tools, The *Playbook* gives them. It feels right. There's no better navigator for your business than one who creatively follows through on a winning instinct.

The other way this vision comes is from the one who created you, directly into your heart. Perhaps this is too heavy for you, but hear me out.

He speaks to us through our hearts and not our minds because the mind reacts too abruptly. Our hearts are much more receptive, passive, and Spirit-led, thus making a better place for him to deliver his instructions. Meditate on this lesson and be obedient to his word, and you'll discover that anything is possible.

This vision of victory in business is similar to the vision parents desire for their kids. We all wish for our children to find success, yet sometimes they don't listen. (Okay, most times.) Recently, I sold a Ford Expedition to former NBA player Melvin Robinson of the Milwaukee Bucks. Melvin is best known for his defense against Dominique Wilkins of the Atlanta Hawks. Melvin's vision for his son, Damion, at that time a seven-foot, four-inch senior at a St. Louis high school, was for him to play professionally in the NBA.

Basketball scouts constantly beat on Damion's door, but he hadn't decided whether basketball was what he wanted to do. "His focus is not clear," Melvin said.

Damion needed someone to instill in him a vision that would navigate him to victory. How many times in your life have you crossed paths with someone who changed your outlook? Pay close attention when this happens. This is when potentially life-changing events will occur. Keep your heart receptive.

Six weeks before graduation, Damion's coach introduced him to a scout who seemed different from the rest. This scout acknowledged that Damion was a gifted young man who was unsure about his future. He was from a major college that had won two championships in the last six years, but you'd never know it by speaking with this low-key man. At the end of the week, he offered Damion a full basketball scholarship, which he accepted.

> *"Your receptive heart will allow you to hear this guidance naturally."*

Melvin asked his son what changed his mind.

"It just felt right, Dad," Damion said.

Imagine the victories you'll have when that still, small voice lets you know that, *this is it*. Your receptive heart will allow you to hear this guidance naturally.

How do you obtain a receptive heart? First you must find a quiet place, like the apostle Peter did when he climbed to the rooftop. Allow yourself a space where you won't be bothered. My beautiful wife, Becky, sometimes sneaks out to our balcony after everyone's asleep, and she sits there in complete silence.

Next, you will need quiet time. Becky leaves her cell phone and all other distractions (our granddaughter, Desiree, and me) in the house. Last, you need to quiet your heart. You accomplish this by relaxing. Put your feet up. Prepare your body as if you were going to sleep. Just before we enter the sleep mode, our hearts relinquish all excess stress. This places the heart in a position to receive the vision. You might begin to fall into a trancelike state. This is how God places your next creative assignment into your heart. Sometimes you will emerge wondering, just like Peter, whether he is sure of his strategy. But it's all part of his wonderful play-calling.

Acts 10:9-20 gives a great example of how God communicated directly to Peter's heart in order to reveal his plan. You'll see that Peter went up on the housetop to pray. Back in those days, the roof was considered the best place for human restoration. The roof was flat and unobstructed, a perfect atmosphere for connecting to God and awaiting his instructions.

The next day, as the messengers from Cornelius were on their journey and coming near the city, Peter went up on the housetop to pray, about the sixth hour. And he became hungry and desired something to eat; but while they were preparing it, he fell into a trance and saw the heaven opened, and something descending, like a great sheet, let down by four corners upon the earth. In it were all kinds of animals and reptiles and birds of the air. And there came a voice to him, "Rise, Peter; kill and eat." But Peter said, "No, Lord; for I have never eaten anything that is common or unclean." And the voice came to him again a second time, "What God has cleansed, you must not call common." This happened three times, and the thing was taken up at once to heaven.

Now while Peter was inwardly perplexed as to what the vision which he had seen might mean, behold, the men that were sent by Cornelius, having made inquiry for Simon's house, stood before the gate and called out to ask whether Simon who was called Peter was lodging there. And while Peter was pondering the vision, the Spirit said to him, "Behold, three men are looking for you. Rise and go down, and accompany them without hesitation; for I have sent them." (Acts 10:9-20)

As the story unfolds, God uses Peter to illustrate how the vision, spoken through the heart, will play a major role in the early church's expansion throughout Galilee and Judea.

A vision is truly a powerful force. We often don't realize its full impact until years later.

For three years, Becky and I were content at our first dealership. My office overlooked a fast food restaurant. The alley behind us led to a convenience store that boasted that it sold more alcohol than coffee between 7:00 and 10:00 in the morning. An adult entertainment establishment named The View Point made up the rest of the block.

Can you imagine the traffic flow between these three businesses? They provided us with several hours of daytime entertainment, certainly better than any television network could come up with. After all, this was live footage.

Business was okay, enough to survive, but that was it. Late in 2002, a vision spoke right into my heart. I was continually steered away from Central Avenue where my dealership was located. Soon I literally could not drive down the street. It began with three weeks of State Fair traffic, then there were traffic accidents, SWAT standoffs, water main breaks, repaving projects, center island landscaping, you name it. I would have no choice but to travel out of my way to Wyoming Boulevard just to run my daily errands. I mean it was to the point of road rage.

Interestingly, it forced me to pass a vacant building that was formerly a Sonic drive-in. Day after day I'd drive by and study this perfect location. I'd get this vision: "What a perfect spot for a used-car lot." Overhangs for all the cars, a drive-around for optimum exposure, and the location was perfect. Kirtland Air Force Base was right down the street.

A week later, the call came. It was the owner of that property, Joe Manning. He called, not to lease me his property, but to sell me some cars he had for sale. Up until then, I had never spoken to Mr. Manning. I told him politely that I wasn't interested in his vehicles, but what about that vacant building on Wyoming? A week later I had a signed six-year lease to the new $5,000 Car Store.

These are those Spirit-led visions that will lead to victory. Follow them without hesitation. With the vision you receive, study the entire playing field. What will it take to win? Imagine you are the coach who seeks only to lead your team to victory. Loss is unacceptable.

After most games, the losing team meets to rehash what went wrong. In their locker room, they scrutinize frame after frame, trying to depict what transpired that resulted in failure.

The winning team, however, looks at things completely differently. A great coach will look at how well his players produced and attempt to improve on how victory was secured.

THE TAKEAWAY: Instill a vision of victory within your team. Do this by individually instilling a vision into each member of your team. You know exactly where they struggle and where they find their joy. You, their coach, can implement this strategy and see the bountiful harvest it produces in the entire team.

CHAPTER 4

PERSEVERANCE KEEPS YOU IN THE GAME

THE DEFENSIVE LINE-UP: It's intimidating and scary. The failure rate among small business start-ups is 70 percent in the first year. After seven years, less than 10 percent of the original businesses will remain in operation.

OFFENSIVE STRATEGY: One of the reasons for this high failure rate is lack of perseverance. Play every day as though it were a championship game with victory in your cross-hairs. Otherwise, defeat will ultimately lead to elimination. With perseverance, you can know the blessing of being a self sufficient, successful small-business owner. To ensure your arrival, practice daily the five play-calls in this chapter. Less than 10 percent of the population resides here. I arrived as a result of my tenacious focus on detail.

◡

Instead of looking up in their time of need, Gabriella Demallo and her three daughters, Rachel, Eva, and Antoinette, looked to Gabriella's mother for direction and moved from their home in Dallas to Corrales, New Mexico. It wasn't exactly what they desired. Rearing her children alone because her husband, Marc, would be incarcerated for the next twenty years, Gabbi realized this move would be difficult for herself and her kids.

Every time she had gotten close to something great, it was snatched away. Therefore, seeing no use in trying to improve the situation, Gabbi decided to stay with her mom and take life as it came. She found a job as a morning shift banquet server at an Albuquerque hotel, where management harassed her and customers tipped lousy and complained bitterly.

A co-worker named Charlene became the only bright spot in the otherwise unfulfilling position. In one of their conversations, Gabbi said that her mother drove her the twenty-five miles to work each morning, tearing her down the entire way. Gabbi desperately needed her own car.

Charlene had purchased a vehicle from the $5,000 Car Store a year earlier. "Go there and Steve will take care of you," she told Gabbi.

Two things usually happen when customers call inquiring about a car. First, they tell their life story. It's ironic how their trials and tribulations are so similar. They sound like discontented nonbelievers: "My ex did this and that. Because of him or her, I'm in this situation."

The customers say they believe, but only when things are

going well. The disconnect occurs when they attempt to do things their way, in their time. They become frustrated, make irrational decisions, and then wonder why things unfold they way they do.

I refer to this lifestyle as the dinner buffet at God's place. You know that famous restaurant located in every city in the world? The great thing about a buffet is that you try only what you like. "I'll try a little Matthew, some James looks good, Corinthians too. Oh, no, not Timothy; that's too spicy. Revelation? I certainly don't need that. It gives me heartburn."

You can't pick and choose his word and will, based on what you like or dislike. It's not about perfection—no one can match that—but it's direction.

When Gabbi called, she told me her life story. Her husband left them without a vehicle, held up some convenience store to satisfy a gambling problem, and on and on. The fact that she needed a car didn't surface, so I asked, "What kind of vehicle are you looking for?"

Next we determined that she was a candidate for our ministry. We set up an appointment, and I let her know what documents were required to purchase the vehicle: a current pay stub, references, and a piece of mail.

Upon her arrival, I learned she didn't have a driver's license. "No problem," I said. "We make them here for only one hundred dollars. Which state would you prefer?"

She laughed at my joke. "My husband did all the driving."

I politely informed Gabbi that before we could do any business, the license issue would have to be resolved. When she began crying hysterically and begging for help, I realized she needed not only a license but a spiritual injection of the Word as well.

Several weeks later with some assistance, Gabbi drove out of our lot. She had her New Mexico driver's license and a nice 2004 Chevy Malibu with great payments, financed in-house.

Seeing her newly restored self-confidence, I later asked her the question that had been on my mind since the first time we spoke. "What would a successful life look like to you?"

"I want to own my own business."

> "What would a successful life look like to you?"

She straightened her spine, gaining an inch in height. "My kids need to learn a different way of living, one that leads to peace, happiness, and prosperity. I just don't know how to get started."

"I know about a book coming out soon that will give you answers. Perhaps until it's available, I can coach you."

She happily agreed. I told her that if she was going to persevere, she would need to surround herself with the right people. This is crucial to success. So often we attempt to go it alone. Or worse, we connect with Satan's influences which are everywhere, seeking out wavering believers.

Growing up in Mendocino County, I grew familiar with the native tree, the redwood. They tower over three hundred feet high and are said to be over two thousand years old. They've weathered many a storm.

You would think that such massive trees would have a root system reaching clear to China. Actually, these giant redwoods have very shallow roots. But, interestingly, they all interlock. In unity, they are unbreakable. When a Pacific Coast storm arrives in December or January with gales over sixty miles per hour, these redwoods barely move.

Why? Because no tree stands alone. All the trees support and protect each other. Sharing the contents of this book with others will foster relationships. It truly is contagious.

Less than one year later, Gabbi and her kids moved back to her hometown, Dallas, and started their own family business. Soon, an e-mail arrived. *How's your book coming? If you don't think it will be successful or you don't finish it, remember my story. The world needs it.*

PERSEVERING THROUGH THE STORM

This chapter will share with you how times of difficulty cause us to persevere through unpleasant interruptions, like a storm that passes through the night and brings the opportunity of a new day.

It's not by luck that some people succeed and others don't. When improperly navigated, they head toward destruction. People who persevere are like an Earl Grey teabag. They produce their best results when exposed to hot water and inconsistent turbulence. Great character emerges in this environment as long as you remain on your prescribed path. Your ability to endure will be tested before you can be promoted.

In August 2008, the top vintners in Napa Valley

concluded that the Cabernet Sauvignon grape harvest was in jeopardy. California's wine production represents 25 percent of the world's harvest. In the Napa Valley Vintner's 2008 report, Chris Howell reported that they had the driest spring in thirty years, and Philippe Melka added that 2008 was a year of harvest extremes.

Luc Morlet had this to say in the same report: "Two consecutive years of drought and a wild spring, toss in a little 'hot' in August, and the result is a substantially lower than normal yield in most vineyards. From a wine making standpoint, the crop reduction was generally regarded as a good thing, as the quality of the grapes benefited dramatically."

The drier soils had allowed the vines to push out early, compensating for the drought condition. The Cabernet harvest of 2008 had the lowest yield in decades, but because the vines struggled, they produced the most colorful and flavorful grapes.

When life's trials and tribulations occur, it's safe to assume that, through perseverance, the outcome can be a better result that one might have thought.

The most difficult aspect of starting a small business is balancing your day job while trying to get your business operational. Over 80 percent of potential small-business owners continue to work their regular paying jobs. Investors are hesitant to lend until they see an established, substantial track record, so there's no other way to secure a future as your own boss.

The $5,000 Car Store was no different. Its heartbeat began at the corner of Candelaria and San Mateo. This is where I met my perspective customers after they answered my advertisement for a vehicle. Looking back, I shudder to think that's where I sold over thirty vehicles in six months.

I soon saw that relocating my temporary car lot was not only a legal matter but also a safety issue. While waiting for one of my customers to show one Saturday, I attracted a man whose picture I recognized from the television: a suspected carjacker. When he walked up, I started the car, anticipating a possible skirmish. He circled the wagon before tapping on my window, waving something in his hand under his coat sleeve. This was my cue for a quick exit.

Stories like this are great to look back on and wonder how I got through them. This is perseverance.

When I worked as a chef, one of the night-shift waiters, Luis, painted houses by day. Entertaining, knowledgeable, and witty, this perfect waiter could barely get to work on time.

Our sympathetic boss, Tony, gave Luis later arrival times to accommodate his self-employment enthusiasm. He'd sometimes show up to work still covered in paint. Most nights, Luis worked until midnight and rose at 5:30 a.m. to pursue his dream.

On Halloween night, Luis didn't bother changing and came as a painter. He juggled his paint brushes eight feet in the air, face-painted the kids, and took home the night's contest, winning two hundred dollars.

A couple of months later, Tony's patience finally expired, and Luis lost his job. He told me the house he was painting on 55th Street produced so many referrals that it resulted in full-time work for the next three months.

Stephanie swapped her day shifts for nights to start her housekeeping business. She worked alone seven days a week, twelve hours a day for over a year before she could afford to hire some help.

"I wanted to quit at least once a month," she said, "but through faith and perseverance I stayed the course."

Today the only day job she has is the one she calls "Stephanie's," her own housekeeping business, employing two people and serving twenty-two clients.

Perseverance isn't sold in a bottle over the counter. Unfortunately, it's something that drives you. This energy will be a net taker of your time for months or years to come. It will distract you from your family, friends, and acquaintances.

Are you prepared to sacrifice and possibly jeopardize these relationships in order to fulfill your dream? Those of you who have established businesses know exactly what I'm talking about. Are your relationships sturdy enough to handle the demands of your calling?

"Quitting my day job will free up a lot of time for those domestic things," the argument goes. Warning: if he has willed you this position in life, you will not have any more time. In fact, you'll probably have less if all goes as planned.

Here are five plays to help you persevere in crafting a successful journey to owning a thriving small business.

NEVER PULL THE TRIGGER
UNTIL YOU'VE CONSULTED EVERYONE IN YOUR CIRCLE

The successful small business is cultivated over several months. You won't snag a great idea on Tuesday and on Saturday open your garage, selling to your first customer. Make sure that all members on your team are on your side. It's also good practice to hire people who offer stimulating ideas. You don't want to employ only those who agree with you, even when you're wrong.

A GREAT PLAY DEVELOPS OVER TIME,
SOMETIMES IN THE LEAST LIKELY OF PLACES

Every month, we invite at least three customers to offer their input to help us better understand the market we serve. They sit in on one of our strategy sessions and offer advice, which we find useful. I'm amazed when I see who sits on the corporate boards of American companies. I never see or hear about a customer who gets the credit for a great idea.

In September 2007, a customer, Yvonne, asked a question during one of our strategy meetings. "If I brought in one of my co-workers, and she purchased a car, would you make my car payment for that month?"

I thought about it for a minute. "If she buys, I'll make the payment. How many co-workers can you bring me?"

It turned out Yvonne made less than half of her twenty-four scheduled car payments. As a result, we initiated our signature customer-referral program. It brings relief to our current customers and adds many new clients to our portfolio.

When a referred customer arrives at the dealership, it's as if she's been here before, because the customer who referred her has already acquainted her with our program and how it works. My dealership operated for six years before we discovered this strategy.

We closed 2009 with 22 percent of our new customers referred by their friends, family, or co-workers. Consider your customers as soldiers on the ground, able to provide great feedback to central command.

FIND SOME REDWOOD TREES

Never go it alone. You won't last long thinking you can do this on your own. My dentist left a successful practice, thinking he'd be better off in his own office. Less than three months later, he was back, saying, "I didn't realize the power in numbers."

Business is all about contacts. The more you have, the better aligned you'll be to gather information and persevere through the storms. I have over three hundred people in my network, and I gladly take the time to entertain input from each one.

ARE YOU IN SHAPE?

The initial impetus of small-business childbirth is excruciating. After the licenses and permits arrive, the commitment has just begun. Be prepared to engage in hours of physical torment. While distributing my stock advisory newsletter, I sacrificed many hours of sleep, preparing the best research I could. That's what separated me from my competitors.

I still work six days a week. The successful small business is a slow process of patience and perseverance. The Halftime chapter gives a brilliant strategy that allows you to maintain this pace.

IS THIS THE RIGHT TIME?

It's true that timing is everything. Only you know when the time is right to make the move from relaxing in your job security to taking the wheel of your own ship called "Destiny." This is huge! You will be the pioneer who had the guts to change your family's directional course. I salute you. God bless you for even thinking this is possible. Your decision to open your own business will change your family's direction for years to come.

Another thought on this subject: Years ago, the family united around the idea of everyone working together in the family business. The farm provided that bond. Today, it's different—or is it? What if you could give an everlasting family heritage to your kids by passing to them a successful small business, which you had the courage to start in the right timing? This could be a great way to restore unity within a family.

THE TAKEAWAY: Persevering through the storms is what separates the failed from the successful, the loser from the champion. The small family business is our only hope for financial freedom and prosperity in this country. Given the current state of our affairs, the family is in trouble. This breakdown results in Satan destroying our kids, which leads to generational disruptions.

If you want to go somewhere you've never been you must have the perseverance to do something you've never done. Uniting in the small family business is one of the best ways we can restore greatness into our culture and take back what was intended for the family. Let's begin today. Formulate a plan to start a family business, and you could help save a generation. The family business is like the redwood trees. Together, nothing can tear us down.

CHAPTER 5

FEED YOUR TEAM

THE DEFENSIVE LINE-UP: Mealtime in corporate America involves a scattering of personnel for at least an hour. This downtime is unproductive and unnecessary. The official time left on the clock after mealtime is far more valuable than one might imagine. How many victories occur in the final minutes of a game? How can you keep your team members together?

OFFENSIVE STRATEGY: Provide an in-house meal the entire team can enjoy. You'll witness miracles unfolding. No kitchen? No problem. I'll show you how to complete over forty satisfying hot and cold meals without a stove, oven, or dishwasher. It's imperative for the team to return tomorrow asking, "What's for lunch?"

～

Food, as we'll see, brings people together and can even produce miracles. A one-hour wait for a table at a spectacular Sunday brunch in a fine Arizona hotel led to a culinary miracle I once saw. I was a waiter there. As I interacted with a family waiting to be seated in my section, I became fond of their matriarch, who was slumped over in her wheelchair.

If you have an elderly person within your family, then you know that a gala event featuring food is equivalent to a child having her tenth birthday at Disneyland. She told me her name was Annie, and she was celebrating her ninety-first birthday. She had been confined to this chair for the past three years because of her unstable legs and a broken hip from a fall.

When their table was ready, the maître d' escorted them thirty yards across the Italian marble floor to the back of the main dining room. Passing by fourteen stations of culinary display, they could just drool.

Once the table was presented to the family's contact and he gave his nod of approval, he pushed Annie up to the table. The family scattered like quail, departing to their favorite culinary stations, leaving Annie completely alone.

But not for long. As I poured the first glass of champagne, Annie rolled her chair back, rose straight up, spurted out a couple of family-related profanities, and strolled across the marble floor.

I couldn't believe my eyes as I witnessed an elderly, wheelchair-bound woman rise up, unassisted, and literally sprint twenty yards across a marble floor to a buffet table. I couldn't let this opportunity slip by unnoticed. To me, it was an inspiring moment. I called attention to this sudden burst of life to everyone in the dining room.

"Ladies and gentlemen, I present to you a miracle, and her name is Annie. She can walk again!"

She received a standing ovation from the 150 patrons who witnessed this miracle. I'm not sure if this made her day or not, but I can tell you, her family was shocked. The majority of the restaurant's patrons stopped eating, rose to their feet, and clapped for what seemed like several minutes.

Annie, with tears streaming down her cheeks, simply said, "It's the wonderful food."

Later that month, a letter arrived at the hotel. In it, Annie's family expressed their gratitude for our excellent service and food.

By the way, the letter concluded by saying that special Sunday was the last time anyone saw Annie walk.

Every small business, whether employing two workers or twenty, encounters a daily point of human breakdown. This occurs while they are thinking about either personal problems or food. Personal problems we'll leave for the psychiatrists.

The time we spend thinking about what we are going to eat for our next meal consumes many productive minutes in most workplaces. Once that decision is made, it's possible that another hour is wasted outside the workplace satisfying the craving.

The solution to this common problem will also help you recognize how you can use food to connect to others within your team.

For example, while muddling through a pre-mealtime Monday, my small staff and I were contemplating an issue that most people spend way too much time deciding: what to eat and where. I suddenly realized I couldn't do this anymore. It was time for a solution. I needed to solve this dilemma by providing a meal for everyone, thus eliminating the time spent thinking about what to eat and, most of all, where.

I faced the same situation that every coach whispers about under his breath. Is it possible that, as head coach, you hold the

> *"Forget raises, bonuses, and those pesky perks. They won't matter anymore..."*
>
> ⌒

key to a universal problem and can solve a daily breakdown? How do you think your team would feel about you and your company if you humbled yourself and prepared them a daily meal at noon? Forget raises, bonuses, and those pesky perks. They won't matter anymore, at least not as much.

You can initiate this technique simply by investing more of your time than your money.

April through September is the ideal time to roll out your new meal program. Begin by purchasing a propane barbeque. Use Friday as the inaugural day, since that is payday for most of you, and your employees' spirits are higher going into the weekend.

I recommend that you and your spouse, partners, or members of senior management participate in the food preparations. This act of humility is an essential key to this program's success.

Make the formal announcement the week before. The message will spread to the entire network of your business. Our business is very spread out. We have three mechanic repair centers, a paint and body facility, detail, emissions, tires, and quality control centers, besides our main collection and sales offices. Each department of service, although close in geographic area, is operated independently. It is impossible to assemble all service personnel to our store at one time, or so we thought. Everyone immediately surprised us when they came together to eat. It's truly amazing how, by offering a quality cooked meal, you can bring everyone together on a voluntary basis at the same time.

Serve the basics. Turkey and beef hamburgers provide a great variety and satisfy almost everyone. Display several varieties of chips and soft drinks and some bottled water.

Be creative with the setting. Here at the $5,000 Car Store, we don't have the luxury of a separate eating facility. When we rolled out our first employee luncheon, we had to work around several of our customers coming in to make payments. Soon space became an issue, so we purchased picnic tables for outdoor eating. Week after week, the natural forces connecting people became clear. The only place to be at noon on Friday was the $5,000 Car Store.

Dan, a driver for one of our auto-part vendors, walked in once during a luncheon. "I deliver to over thirty businesses every day. This one is different," he said.

"Why is that?" I asked.

"I get the feeling that everyone who walks in here is welcome," Dan said. "Usually, I get in and out as fast as possible and don't talk to anyone. Drop the delivery, get a signature, and leave. But I don't want to leave this place. And you serve your people lunch too?"

He joined us for lunch. While he ate, he gave us some inside knowledge. We found out who to speak to in order to receive our parts within an hour of placing our order.

The next Friday, I received a call from the neighboring Dodge dealership. It was Don, the parts manager, asking what was on the menu that day. I thought he was joking, but he wasn't. How did he hear about our lunch program?

After his first lunch with us, our Dodge service suddenly changed status. They gave us the code name "hemi," which meant we would receive same-day service. They also gave us a new price structure, which was very favorable, compared to our old one.

One Friday, I was preparing the condiments in the back room when one of our customers happened by on her way to the restroom. With a curious expression she asked, "What's for lunch?"

"Barbequed chicken and potato salad," I said. "Can you stay?"

She couldn't resist. That Friday, we offered lunch to every customer who made a payment during lunch hour.

On one occasion I was running late, so I ordered pizza. The driver who delivered that day was looking for a car. He didn't think he could afford one due to his poor credit score and a recent, bitter breakup that left him with less income than before.

He ended up purchasing a car a week later and referred

three of his friends. Whenever I drive by this pizza restaurant and my four cars are parked out in front, I'm blessed to see this further evidence that food miracles really can make a difference.

In addition to the barbeque, we invested in a camping stove and small propane burners, which have allowed us to prepare many different hot meals.

Three local shops service our vehicles. One of these shops brazenly delivered a serviced vehicle right at lunchtime one Friday. The entire staff, six people, emptied out of our PT Cruiser, asking "What's for lunch?"

At first this presented an awkward dilemma. Would we have enough food? It wasn't as if I could look up into the sky and ask the Father to turn three chickens into ten. This miracle is best left to someone else.

However, it did occur to me that this could develop into a fantastic food miracle. I rushed next door to McDonald's and brought back the "happy meal deal," all six of them.

We now invite our entire team to lunch. A good mechanic can be a rock star when it comes to performing miracles on your vehicle. These informal gatherings give customers an excellent opportunity to get to know those miracle workers, off the clock and in an environment where they are free to converse. Outside at our picnic tables during lunchtime, we often witness these mechanical surgeons interacting with our customers as if they are family. My dear friends, this is the miracle of food.

At our stores, the service personnel offer advice, set appointments, and answer customers' questions while they eat their lunch. Can you imagine how special our customers feel? Each one feels important. Most have met all the service players, and we quickly introduce the new ones when the customers come to make their payments conveniently while lunch is served.

Can you visualize how this play might fit into your game plan to enhance the culture of your business? We now serve lunch three to four times a week. As a side benefit, one of my general managers has lost forty-five pounds.

Every business must justify all its expenses. This new accounting entry, labeled "Feed the Team," is one reason why, month after month, our customers make their payments on time. We have the lowest delinquent-payment rates in the nation, less than 10 percent, for the subprime market. An acquaintance of mine, a banker who caters to a much more affluent market, is content when his numbers are well above this.

No one is excluded because you never know who will benefit next. Something happens at this business that sets it apart from the rest. It's not just a business; it's a ministry that's coached as though it were a championship team.

I believe this concept can work within any type of business. A miracle occurs when you humble yourself and feed the people who care about your company's success. This will produce a satisfying return that will far outweigh your financial investment. If it can make a crippled, ninety-one-year-old woman walk again, imagine what it could do for your business.

The Workplace Cookbook, a companion to the *Playbook*,

available soon, contains forty recipes you can prepare in less than an hour. These spiritually satisfying meals fill your team's most important needs, build relationships with your customers, and create unique partnerships with your suppliers.

THE TAKEAWAY: Humble yourself and bring your entire team together for one big huddle. This stimulating setting will produce ideas that flow through these wonderful players who help create your success.

CHAPTER 6

AVOID THE PENALTY, NO FLAG

THE DEFENSIVE LINE-UP: The infamous safety blitz comes at you from both sides of the field. Its frivolous claims of impropriety, wrongdoing, product liability, and false charges challenge your integrity.

OFFENSIVE STRATEGY: We must honor and respect those in authority, even though some who hold those positions may not be honorable. We'll present the best offense we can and hope they will seek easier prey.

⤳

Let every person be subject to the governing authorities. For there is no authority except from God, and those that exist have been instituted by God. Therefore he who resists the authorities resists what God has appointed, and those who resist will incur judgment. For rulers are not a terror to good conduct, but to bad. Would you have no fear of him who is in authority? Then do what is good, and you will receive his approval, for he is God's servant for your good. But if you do wrong, be afraid, for he does not bear the sword in vain; he is the servant of God to execute his wrath on the wrongdoer. Therefore one must be subject; not only to avoid God's wrath but also for the sake of conscience. For the same reason you also pay taxes, for the authorities are ministers of God, attending to this very thing. Pay all of them their dues, taxes to whom taxes are due, revenue to whom revenue is due, respect to whom respect is due, honor to whom honor is due. (Romans 13:1-7)

⌐

The three things adults fear most are public speaking, parachuting out of an airplane at twelve thousand feet, and a visit from the Internal Revenue Service.

The call on hold for me was from Beth Ryan Anderson. I wasn't too disturbed about receiving a call from someone I didn't recognize, since this happens on a regular basis. I hung up the other line and picked up the call from Ms. Anderson.

She introduced herself as an IRS agent here in Albuquerque. "You've been selected to receive an audit for the fiscal year 2005."

Sure I have. Who put you up to this? I'd always heard

that the IRS notifies by certified mail. Stressful news always arrives by mail.

Ms. Anderson insisted on an appointment to come to my dealership and conduct her audit. I went along with her request, and we scheduled a meeting for about three weeks later.

After I hung up the phone, I sat back in my chair, wondering who was behind this prank. Was it Chuck Nunson, a friend who works for one of those big dealerships? I had his pride and joy towed away while he was having lunch at Pancho's New Mexican Restaurant about a week prior to this. His 2005 250-horsepower BMW 330 CI Sport Coupe went missing for about an hour.

This was in retaliation for the time he sent a customer to me and convinced her to pretend to be someone I knew. Chuck had fed this lady all kinds of information about me that only a few people who'd worked with me would have known. She played me like a fiddle for at least thirty minutes, convincing me that we had worked together some ten years before. She could have received an award for her performance. I couldn't for the life of me figure out who she was. About an hour after she left, Chuck called, laughing, reminding me that "we shouldn't make a practice of wasting time trying to sell cars to people we used to work with."

Or perhaps it was someone here at the $5,000 Car Store. We're always making things interesting around here. Recently, I had placed a briefcase filled with $3000 in cash with a fake handgun, handwritten demand note, and a ski mask barely sticking out from under the driver's side seat of the 2003 Olds Alero that Juan Carlos was detailing. He raced into the lobby with this case, and his face held more disbelief than I've ever seen. It still makes me laugh every time I think about it.

The next thing I did was to call the Albuquerque IRS office to verify the authenticity of this agent and the validity of her call. Sure enough, Beth Ryan Anderson was an auditor there, and my appointment was on official record.

Wow! What do I do now? A letter of explanation and instructions arrived a few days later. I let my family and friends know what was going on, and they reacted with fear, anger, and anxiety.

I wasn't worried. I had been coached by some pretty great teachers—those New Testament fellows. They taught me to keep great records, do it myself, do it right, and always be prepared. You never know when you'll have to display your personal records of account- ability and compli-

> *"...lack of compliance is one of the most common reasons many small businesses fail."*

ance. This review, as they like to refer to it, was going to con- sume two business days, so I should make myself available and be punctual, the letter said.

On the appointed day, Ms. Anderson pulled into my dealership in a late-model Mercedes-Benz sedan with no driver's side mirror. That was interesting.

She reached into her trunk and pulled out the latest technologically advanced laptop and printer. Smiling, she introduced herself as Agent Anderson. She informed me that the first step in this process was to compile a company profile, which would take about three hours to complete.

Thirty minutes later, we finished the profile and adjourned to my back office for that wonderful compliance examination, described by many as "the most stressful two days of your life." At this point, I have to tell you, I was completely at peace. I had conducted myself the way I believe any servant-style coach would if he were running this small business. This confirmed the "practice what you preach" doctrine.

As a testimony to this, Agent Anderson finished her assignment and left before lunch on the first day with no amendments to my return.

I asked her about that missing side mirror (noncompliant, illegal, and dangerous).

She shot a glance toward the driver's side door. "It's been like that for three months."

DEALING WITH GOVERNING BODIES

This chapter will strengthen your views of the governing bodies we have to comply with. It will prepare you to deal with them and overcome any challenges that arise due to their potential abuse of power.

Other than Spirit Capital, lack of compliance is one of the most common reasons many small businesses fail.

You can interact with compliance authorities in one of two ways: either fight them or present yourself as a submissive business owner who wishes only to comply.

At my first location, a man named Tony owned the drive-in next to us. He was always undertaking small but tedious construction projects. Sidewalks, overhangs, lighting, signs, handicap painting, menu box adjustments, landscape trimming—at first glance, you would have thought he was a proud business owner who wished the best for his property.

But the fact was that the city's enforcement vehicle, that shiny Ford Ranger, pulled in there more often than some of his regular lunch customers. Tony's personality produced this type of result. I saw him on multiple occasions when he came to work in the mornings and threw out homeless people who sought refuge overnight in his dumpsters. The way he treated his staff and his complaining customers—it all added up. The officials in charge of his compliance received the same treatment. Submissive he was not; penalized severely, he was.

I believe the best defense is a great offense. None of us enjoy having someone with that much power watching over us, except maybe the two men in heaven who sit side by side. That should be enough; but unfortunately, we need others to keep us in check. If you are contemplating starting a new business or have one, the most important thing you can do to ward off an invasion of the governing authorities is to present an attitude of submissiveness. It's all in the look. Does your company look compliant?

You may think you have too much oversight already. These servants of municipal intrigue don't have a clue about your business. Yet they are responsible for enforcing the laws governing your business. Give me a break.

I understand how you feel. A car dealership has to be

one of the most cumbersome businesses when it comes to compliance. The paper trail alone damages the world's tree population, and that's a real problem for me. Having said this, I still emphasize maintaining an aggressive offense when displaying the exterior of your business to the public.

Your business may be wholesale, retail, or home-based. Regardless, you will still have to comply with government authorities as well as moral ones.

I used to pick up my own parts from a dealership warehouse that, ironically, is no longer in business. Granted, this warehouse was behind the dealership and not visible from the street. I had to run an obstacle course just to enter through the front door. Inside, the centerfold pictures on the wall and the remnants of last night's five-table poker game gave the impression that no one there upheld any standards except those Satan would endorse. The staff of the $5,000 Car Store knows that our stores are the stage on which we perform.

Lord knows, our only objective here is to be on the offensive. "That foul odor, officer, couldn't originate from our store. It's coming from over there." Let's keep this officer from ever pulling into your place of business. We do this by presenting an exterior that shouts, "I'm compliant."

Here are six techniques we use daily to combat the enforcers so that they pursue easier prey.

THE PLAYING FIELD

Any vehicle in my inventory can begin leaking at any time. Just ask Juan Carlos. These things are full of fluids.

Leaks are one issue the enforcers look for, so we never allow a vehicle to sit parked on our lot with a fluid leak underneath. Instead, we move and dust daily each vehicle then spray the interior with refreshing cologne.

Your entrance is the gateway to your personality. This is how your customers will perceive what business you offer and how you conduct it. The entrance of the McDonald's next door is a morning meeting place for every pigeon in the area. You can only imagine the moves you must endure to avoid their presence, just to walk through the door. This store boasts that they have the cleanest public restrooms in town, but getting to them may be a bit sticky.

On the other hand, the Taxation and Revenue officer who thought he had a rift with me, after looking around my building, immediately realized we were a compliant operation.

THE CANDY COLLECTION: IT'S THE LITTLE THINGS

We keep several varieties of complimentary candy on display. Anyone who has ever been inside our lobby knows to veer right first and grab the day's offering before conducting business. Give your business' entry the feel of your home, allowing your personality to exude. Let everyone who enters feel welcome. The fire marshal from Station Number Five, who conducts my annual inspection, says the same thing every year. "On the outside, your place looks like a car lot, but the inside feels like someone's living room."

PROPER POSTINGS OF REQUIRED DOCUMENTATION

My dealership was once ambushed by the New Mexico State Police. That Thursday afternoon, my lobby looked like a SWAT convention. We sold a vehicle that was carjacked soon after delivery. The nice people arrested implicated us as collaborators in the crime.

When New Mexico's finest theft recovery unit bombarded our dealership, they quickly discovered that our business could never have had anything to do with this horrible crime. One reason was that we had displayed our business license, fee schedules, privacy policies, mission statement, etc. in matching frames for all to see. I also hung every required federal posting, such as worker's compensation and minimum wage flyers, in the back office, which the authorities could plainly see.

A little effort will produce a professional first impression that this business respects authority.

YOUR SCOREBOARD

I don't believe it's ever prudent to post your political preferences, grievances, or opinions along your property. There are many reasons for this, the most important being the Bible's take on the subject. There is no room for negative attitudes within the body of Christ. Since we want the ministry to define our business model, we opt to forgo the controversial.

On one of the windiest March days in Albuquerque's history, I was determined to add another sign affiliation to my building. I purchased two eight-foot two-by-fours, made the proper cuts, fashioned a cross, and painted it white. Despite wind gusts of sixty to sixty-five miles per hour, I hung the most beautiful eight-foot cross from the top of my building. If I leave the dealership after dark, I will go out of my way just to drive by and see "Him" lit up. I've never witnessed another non-church business owner express love for Christ in this manner.

It's time to give a public testimony to the reason we're successful. If you're not doing this yet, perhaps it's time to start.

LOVE THIS COUNTRY

Our property allows us to display the American flag throughout our front fence line. I purchased six ten-foot PVC pipes, drilled the proper holes, and wire-strung flags through the two grommets. Anchored six feet apart, these three-by-five-foot American flags proudly stand for the great love we share for our country. A tourist from another country could drive by and confuse us with the American embassy.

NO NEED TO COOK THE BOOKS; A LITTLE SIMMERING WILL SUFFICE

When the IRS contacted me, I called my CPA in California. The only service he provides for me is preparing my year-end tax material. When I told him what was going on, he immediately began to arm me with the legal weapons within his arsenal. They included a very expensive tax attorney, an IRS audit counselor, and others to help us defend ourselves against these regulators.

My dear friends, having witnessed firsthand the scrutiny of an IRS audit, my conclusion is simple: the images you reflect determine the results you receive. You don't need to hire these high-dollar masterminds. First of all, no one except you should ever calculate or prepare your business records. Do not subcontract this weighty responsibility.

Revenues at the $5,000 Car Store will exceed four million dollars this year, along with over 700 delivered vehicles, all without the assistance of a bookkeeper. I'm still the only one who works with my books. If you wish to learn how to keep excellent records, I suggest you attend one of my free workshops so you can learn to apply financial accountability to your business, using Christian principles.

Almost every tax audit and compliance issue brought against your business is created by the lack of compliance awareness. You can easily avoid problems by implementing some risk management.

Risk management begins with how people perceive your business. Ask yourself the question: Looking at my stage right now, am I satisfied in knowing I've taken every possible step to ward off danger? Compliance is a reality we business owners have to live with. If we choose to ignore it, legal issues can arise.

The used-car industry ranks within the top ten types of businesses involved in lawsuits in this country.

THE TAKEAWAY: The estimated time in which a small business can expect to be approached by a legal challenge is three years. After nine years, we have just been served our first lawsuit: Corely vs. $5000 Car Store, LLC. What began as a frivolous inquiry into our disclosure practices soon dissolved as a local dealership attack attorney discovering that this company had its compliance with the law in order. The outcome was a substantially lowered expectation by the plaintiff. Sorry, Ms. Corely; perhaps next time you and your legal team will seek a less-compliant business for your frivolous suit.

CHAPTER 7

GIFTS ARE PLAYS SENT FROM ABOVE

THE DEFENSIVE LINE-UP: How will I know what my true gifts are? Will they be powerful enough to lead me to success in my business?

OFEENSIVE STRATEGY: Many of us ponder these questions but fail to explore their true meaning. Imagine taking a journey in which you know your destination with precise accuracy. Through gifted energy, you were created to serve a purpose. Discover your gift and learn to implement this energy into a successful life. It's what separates the champions from the mediocre.

Nestled within ninety feet of ocean cliffs, two hundred miles north of San Francisco, lies the small town of Mendocino, California. Late summer is the perfect time to make the trip. It's when the grape harvest is in full swing along State Highway 128.

Along fifty-eight miles of twisting and turning two-way traffic, you pray no one crosses the double yellow lines. Thirty-one wineries compete for your attention, their decorative signs praising their award-winning vintages. Should you stop and experience the grapes, it surely helps ease the winding road that seems never to end.

> *"Did you ever dream this was possible?"*

Towering two-thousand-year-old redwoods form a shadow-filled backdrop as you climb the last thirteen miles through the dark Jackson State Park forest. At last, the scent of sea air wafts in as you climb straight up the last hill to the top of northbound Highway One. Look to your left, and the magnificent Pacific Ocean captures your breath.

Dick Scobee and his wife, June, journeyed that route to see us for dinner one night back in 1984. Much of the dining conversation centered around Dick's description of his recent NASA mission. In April, he had piloted *Challenger* mission STS-41-C, which successfully deployed one satellite and repaired another.

Sitting next to my mom, who worked in the pre-Apollo

space industry. She asked him, "Dick, do you realize where you've been? Did you ever dream this was possible?"

His reply was the one he often used when someone asked how to get started in the space industry. "When you discover something you really like to do, and you are willing to risk its consequences, and it's in your heart, you ought to do it. Realize that it's a gift given to you exclusively."

The world would come to know that Lieutenant Colonel Dick Scobee did receive his blessed gift and made the ultimate sacrifice. He became the commander of *Challenger* mission STS-51-L, which suffered catastrophic booster failure and exploded seventy-three seconds into flight on January 28, 1986.

Several months after his death, I read a handwritten letter that his daughter, Kathie, wrote describing her father. Its conclusion read, "My father died doing exactly what he was destined to do."

His 1984 mission patch, which he wore on his uniform shoulder, is framed and hangs proudly on my office wall.

We often wonder why the Father grants such wonderful gifts to people so willing to receive them when their outcome renders devastation. I have many theories as to why this happens. My best explanation is that because of this horrible misfortune, we can thank a gifted believer like Dick Scobee. His sacrifice remedied a serious internal problem at NASA that has never occurred again.

Like Commander Scobee, you will find fulfillment when you pursue this formula: know which gifts God has blessed you with, unleash this bountiful energy, and discover how your gifts will serve others. With these three forces at work, your small business will flourish, because you will have exceeded your customers' expectations.

These gifts become the blueprint for the rest of your life. It would make perfect sense to become familiar with this supernatural, energy so that you can fulfill the purpose he has destined for you.

Begin by searching your heart. This is where you will discover what drives you. You have inside you a relentless energy that you burn without trepidation. If you experience doubt, it's only because in your mind you haven't yet drafted an assignment that exercises this energy.

Ever since I can remember, I was drawn to the lower-middle-class population. Through the years, I have developed a real passion for these people. After all, I was one of them. Most are genuine, hardworking, and honest. Since I was young, I have continually sought ways to make their lives better.

Be aware of what can happen when our inherent nature lures us in different directions while we search out our gifted energy. Navigating away from the epicenter of the energy that drives you always results in failure. It's okay to attempt new things, but beware of distractions that disconnect you from your purpose.

Whenever my efforts drew me away from this zone, things in my life didn't work well. Real estate investing and day stock trading, before it was fashionable, were wonderful experiences but left me incomplete when the day was done. It became clear that he kept placing me in readiness to serve these people. This was my gifted assignment. He placed enough clues in my path to convince me that this was where I belong.

I never in a million years thought I would be assisting this group of people with their transportation needs. When I informed my mother that I'd be starting a small business selling used cars, she was shocked. In truth, she wasn't much more surprised than I was by this decision.

After he blessed our business for ten years, we set a goal to have ten stores in three states by the year 2012. My gift of serving people's needs has evolved throughout my life as I used these three dynamics: realize the gift, know how to set this supernatural energy to work, and give service to others. If you manage your small business with this knowledge, you will succeed beyond your wildest dreams. This is how we know an unexplainable force is leading us.

Your small business is truly the reflection of your personality. Its early success depends on whether you apply your bestowed, gifted energy to serving your customers. The number one reason most small businesses fail is because the owners do not pursue the business with gifted energy. Rather, they begin with a hobby or a fad, reflective of current events.

My good friend, Sandy, started a daycare business in the early eighties because so many people were talking about the employment shift within the economy. Sandy thought this anecdotal strategy would create a huge market for child daycare. The assumption proved correct. With moms and dads both working, her business model flourished.

But she failed within the first year. I believe this happened because daycare wasn't her blessed gift. She pursued something with huge potential, but the internal forces—the gift, the implementation, and service to others—were not present within her heart. She pursued a fad.

Sandy returned to her day job as a gifted golf instructor. Seven months later, she became the pro.

> "A gift is granted to you supernaturally and given for the purpose of serving others."

My Sacramento neighbor, John Ramsey, was perplexed that his business failed in its first ten months. Everyone told him he could cook barbeque better than anyone, and I agreed. I knew whenever I smelled smoke coming from his backyard, that I'd better place my order, now. When John barbequed, ten to fifteen cars always parked outside his home, waiting to purchase the daily special. We all agreed that his flavorful sauces and unique style of smoking meat would help him have a successful barbeque restaurant. It truly was his passion.

Why did he fail? I believe it's because barbequing was just his hobby and not a gift.

What's the difference? A hobby is a leisurely pastime that provides for personal fulfillment and relaxation, not to be confused with a Spirit-led journey that he lays out for us.

If you can't differentiate between the two, you can always use this guide. A gift is granted to you supernaturally and given for the purpose of serving others. When properly executed, it's a guaranteed path to success. A hobby, however, is

THE PLAYBOOK *for* SMALL BUSINESSES

used for the sole purpose of giving personal satisfaction and is a recipe for business failure.

Your spiritual gifts come to you at birth. These are natural energies that allow you to accomplish with ease and grace what you put your mind to. My friend, Mike Gallarda, recalls his classmates looking over his shoulder while he drew pictures in the fourth-grade classroom. Every kid wanted his drawings. He knew then that he had a gift. If you Google his name, you will see he is an internationally-renowned trompe l'oeil artist who has exhibited paintings on display in galleries in London, New York, and Santa Fe. The *Playbook's* cover is a good example of his work.

God constantly tugs you in the direction he deems best, leaving clues along the path. In my example, he allowed me to try other things. Successful as they were, they were not his will for my life. I knew this because of the emptiness I felt even after several victories. The loneliness inside told me instinctively that I was not aligned with the Father's will.

Are you serving others with your gifted energy?

Your successes should be made known to all, for it is not yourself but he who navigates you. Share your great fortune with all who inquire. You will be successful in your pursuits when you explain the reason for that success. I believe few people understand this concept; as a result, over thirty thousand businesses fail in this country every month.

If you currently own or are contemplating starting a small business, define your gifted energy, use it to accomplish great works, and serve others. Then you will bear witness to an amazing life that leads to success.

THE TAKEAWAY: The realization of the gift: At age fourteen, I had just landed my first job as a dishwasher at a local restaurant. Perched in my lonely corner, I scrutinized the chefs as they flipped those skillets full of culinary morsels. The head chef, Peter, could flip a skillet of scallops five feet in the air without ever losing one. They were all great entertainers, putting on a show as the restaurant's patrons strolled through, led by the hostess, to their reserved tables.

Whenever the opportunity allowed, I raced through the chefs' formation, picking up their used pots and pans. One day I braved my fear. Scrambling through a routine pickup, with my left hand full of used pots, my right hand grabbed one of those skillets on the stove and flipped the order of scampi perfectly.

Peter saw this. "Pretty fancy there, boy. Do you want to cover a shift this Friday?"

Of course I did. The fascinating thing about gift discovery is not whether it will happen, but when it will happen. It's usually when you least expect it.

Was this my gift? After three weeks, it became obvious I belonged in front of the stove. My dishwashing career had come to an end. The effortless, exciting, and fulfilling energy I felt every time I strode into that kitchen showed me that the culinary field was exactly where I was supposed to be.

Four months later, on New Year's Eve, Peter walked out the service door without giving notice and climbed into a car, and was gone. With dinner tickets piling up, the entire staff realized it was just me and two other cooks. The busiest night of the year was only half over, and our plane was flying without its pilot. However, if you happened to be a dinner guest at the Sea Gull Inn that evening, you would never have guessed that the rest of the night's show was led by a gifted fifteen-year-old.

A rookie quarterback may sit on the bench for years, taking snaps only in preseason. But when the big opportunity arrives, he must be prepared. This play, called in from above, will probably come only once. Let's be ready.

The implementation: A year later, a drunken idiot left his cigarette smoldering in an overstuffed chair in the Sea Gull Inn's lounge. My gifted dream vanished in smoke as the inn burned to the ground. Funny thing, right next door was the Mendocino Volunteer Fire Department.

Would I receive another job offer in this small coastal town? The owner, David Jones, vowed to rebuild. A month later, I received a call from the Little River Inn, asking whether I was interested in a prep-cook position. Although I knew the Gull wouldn't re-open for several months, I accepted. The kitchen was beyond anything I had seen. There were sauces and entrees I couldn't even pronounce, let alone prepare.

Your gifts and the possibilities for achievement will become clear to you if you pursue them with confidence instead of trepidation. Led by an energy that I couldn't have possessed at sixteen, I took the controls. Five months later, I became the youngest head chef in the Little River Inn's sixty-year history. This, my friends, is exactly what Colonel Scobee spoke of when he said, "When you discover something you really like to do, and you are willing to risk its consequences, and it's in your heart, you ought to do it."

Persevering through challenges will reveal and confirm your gifts. Then you'll be able to overcome any obstacles that stand in your way. Pursue and implement them. You'll soon discover whether they're real or not.

The service or product you choose to pursue through the application of gifted energy will allow you to succeed beyond your wildest of dreams. However, don't think it all ends there. If you desire to reach the pinnacle of success, give back that supernatural power that flows through you to others. This ministry will lead to a climatic destination. My hope is that someday everyone who has applied this winning formula will experience its beauty.

CHAPTER 8

NOT ALL PLAYERS ARE EQUAL

THE DEFENSIVE LINE-UP: New Mexico has over twelve hundred car dealerships. How can you separate yourself from the herd when the numbers appear to be stacked against you? Will your business face these odds too? The answer is yes.

OFFENSIVE STRATEGY: Establishing your own unique brand in a competitive environment will not be enough to ward off failure. Your brand recognition must exceed the expectations of your customers. You make this possible by reaching out to your customers and exceeding their experience with what you offer. Victory follows when you show them that not all businesses are created equal.

‿

When Tiffany Harrison called me from the new car dealership, her voice held the unmistakable tones of distress. I got this much before someone grabbed the phone and hung up.

Tiffany had traded in her vehicle and bought a new one from a new car dealership. To her dismay, the bank financed loan fell though, and now the dealership wanted their car back.

But there was a problem. The sale had been completed three and a half weeks ago, her trade-in had been sold to a wholesaler, and no finance company would extend credit to her.

Tiffany was a victim of dealership spot delivery, the sale of a vehicle with only the assumption of a loan, not approval. This can result in the failure to obtain financing after the vehicle has been delivered. A creative way for larger dealerships to sell thousands of vehicles, spot delivery carries the danger of a rejected loan application. Then what?

When Tiffany and her boyfriend drove home in their new 2007 vehicle, costing over sixteen thousand dollars, they had left their trade-in vehicle and down payment behind. They believed the story those financial henchmen from the dealership told them: "Everything is fantastic. Don't worry about a thing."

Tiffany began to worry when her thirty-day temporary plate was about to expire, thus requiring her to get a permanent license plate and registration. Worry turned to panic when the dealer contacted her to explain the unfortunate financial circumstance that had developed. He advised her to bring the vehicle back.

When she returned to the dealership, she discovered she never had been financed. Her trade-in, a 2002 Hyundai Elantra that she purchased and paid for in full at the $5,000 Car Store, was nowhere to be found.

> *"...not every team is equally coached."*
>
> ⤳

What happened next is truly hard to believe. Tiffany was literally held against her will as the dealer attempted to reconcile with her. In an attempt to appease her, they pulled out all the stops: eight different vehicles to choose from, rebates, discounts, free service warranties, pizza delivery—nothing made her cave in.

They refused to let her leave before they were sure she would drive home in another of their cars of much lesser value. Nine different dealership employees attempted to break her without success. Five hours elapsed, then she made a run for it.

Later that week, Tiffany retained an attorney. She was appalled to hear that the dealership had closed its doors forever, part and parcel, due to the bankruptcy filing of General Motors. Tiffany returned to the $5,000 Car Store and purchased another vehicle.

Everyone is equal except when it comes to business. Tiffany learned, as you will in this chapter, that not every team is equally coached.

From Ordinary to Extraordinary

This chapter reveals several tips on how to exceed your customers' expectations and elevate your business from ordinary to extraordinary.

As humans, we are created equally by God. For now, we are judged by our customers. Listen to them, for they determine whether your business is a success or a failure.

Here are some observations and solutions I've collected over time. They deserve some consideration, and I believe you'll find them insightful.

EXCEED EXPECTATIONS

Jesus told a parable about a sower scattering seed and how it might result in a large or small harvest or produce nothing at all. One lesson we can glean is that our efforts produce different results, depending on how people respond. This is exactly how I see business today. It's how your customers see it too. Let's lead them to the fertile soil, detouring away from a secular mind-set, so we can reap a plentiful harvest.

My customers are no different from yours. They are equal in the sense that they expect to be respected, treated fairly, and satisfied with their purchase when exiting your business.

But how about exceeding this perception? What if your customers left your place of business feeling surprised that someone would respect them enough to spend adequate time exceeding their expectations? This simple yet complex concept separates success from failure. It begins with something free—your time. This has completely disappeared from today's business climate. As a business leader, I'm confident that once customers are familiar with our culture, they will be reluctant to return to the treatment they tolerated from our competitors.

FIRST POINT OF CONTACT

Your customers' introduction to your business is crucial. They want to know what you have to offer and how you offer it. Do you have a standard protocol for fulfilling this request?

When I call my favorite pizza restaurant, I get the same response every time: "Gaucho's Pizza, please hold!"

I love their pizza. One of their toppings is a homemade roasted green chili with garlic and olive oil. Do you think they're going to lose my business because I have to wait three minutes before receiving service? Probably not, but this isn't exceeding my expectations either. It's merely ordinary.

We endure the same challenge at the $5,000 Car Store. Things get extremely busy because of our no-appointment policy. Servicing this volume at peak times is difficult; yet without a doubt, it's the most crucial personal contact my business encounters.

I know Pete and Cecilia, the owners of Gaucho's, very well, so I suggested a plan to them. For every minute their valued customer waits on hold for a representative to take the pizza order, she gets one dollar shaved from her bill. Sounds ridiculous, doesn't it?

One of two things is going to happen. Either their customers will receive several dollars of reduced pizza costs during peak hours, or the people answering the phones at Gaucho's won't place their customers on hold, because management creatively solved this problem.

The answer was to install two separate phone lines, one for carryout and one for delivery. On Friday nights, Pete and Cecilia offer the dollar giveaway. Business on that night has increased 20 percent, year over year. They won't tell me how many pizza dollars they give away, though.

NEW CUSTOMER SERVICE
EMERGES FROM AN OLD PROBLEM

We use Miguel's Tire Shop on Central Avenue. On the average, we spend six hundred dollars a week there.

Miguel and his employees are created equal, but his service is not. At lunchtime, you can expect him to have my "Chapter Five" up and running. Being of Hispanic descent, he serves tamales, chile rellenos, tacos, enchiladas, taquitos, a pot of beans, or a specialty dish. I would wager he serves a better meal than most Mexican restaurants in the area.

What I like about Miguel's service is the fact that I never need an appointment. His customers drop off their vehicles, and he delivers them with new tires, balanced and rotated, back to their homes or businesses at no charge.

He's never advertised and there's always a wait at his shop. One day, Juan got tired of circling Miguel's little driveway on the corner of Central and Vermont. He decided to leave the vehicle and walk back to the dealership. We let Miguel know about the problem. Thus his pickup-and-delivery service was born.

DISCOVER YOUR CLIENTS' NEEDS

If I had to advertise, I'd spend somewhere in the neighborhood of three thousand dollars a month. That's the amount my competition spends for their pictorials in the car magazines. When you advertise, there's no guarantee of results. The ad executives make that disclaimer clear when you place your order.

Wouldn't it be prudent to take those dollars you've earmarked for angling new customers and apply them back into your existing customer base instead? If you assist them in their time of need, they will be your source of advertisement. The best ad I've ever seen is a customer sharing his outstanding experience with a friend, family member, or co-worker.

Our business model allows me to purchase only used vehicles that often require repairs. Car trouble is a permanent part of the used-car business. When one of my customers is in need of a repair, the reality is they probably won't have the money to fix it.

But they know Steve is there for them. You can read the results of this effort on our Internet reviews. We receive more referrals because of this single issue than we do from our low payments, great cars, friendly service, convenient locations, or willingness to sell anyone a vehicle.

Select an area within your business that could be a direct

link to exceeding your customers' expectations. Focus on it, and you'll see an immediate impact. Customers love to talk to one another about a great experience. Equally, they will slam a bad one if they have reason.

I don't know of another dealer willing to repair their customers' vehicles before, during, and well after the sale the way we do. We'd rather use this money directly at the source, targeting the bull's-eye. The result of this effort is conclusive. We've never advertised for new business.

JUST ANOTHER NUMBER?

When I enter the salon where I get my hair cut, the pretty, young hostess asks not for my name but my phone number. For a man of my age with very few hairs left, this is flattering, and I have to smile. Certainly it's her job, but it's so impersonal.

On a recent visit there, I asked who the owner was. Cindy, who often cuts my hair, wrote her name on the back of her business card. Visibly sensing a problem, she asked me why I was interested.

"While we sit here getting our hair cut, we're a captive audience. You have a great opportunity to enhance your culture in hopes of gaining referrals, which must form a large part of your business."

Cindy looked back at me in the mirror, and her wide, blank eyes told me she wasn't getting it.

"You know that I'm married and we're raising our grand-daughter who attends the elementary school practically next door," I said, ticking off the items on my fingers. "I own a business, have several rental properties, and take Sundays off. I've told you all this before, yet you don't use this information to improve upon our relationship. If you did, I'd leave here wanting to tell my friends and family members about this friendly salon."

Neither Becky, Desi, or any of our neighbors get their hair cut at this salon. If the employees would remember my name and show an interest in me, they would exceed my expectations. I would willingly tell everyone about this salon less than two miles from our home.

With very few hairs left on the top of my head, it's not about the haircut. Everyone desires to feel more important than just another number, right?

MAKE YOUR PRODUCT ATTRACTIVE

While running into a Wal-Mart, I saw a squad of high-school cheerleaders, complete with uniforms, at the entrance. My first thought was to sneak in behind someone and thereby skirt the challenge of saying, "No, thank you," to a student who was trying to raise money for a school activity.

Instead, I approached their display and found that they were selling different flavors of popcorn sealed in microwave-ready pouches. Their school's insignia, name, and colors decorated each bag. Someone had spent a lot of time and money designing these. The only problem was that sales were flat and time was limited, since Wal-Mart allows fundraisers at only one entrance for one hour. No one seemed the least bit interested in buying popcorn right before the dinner hour.

God constantly places me in these situations, and I feel I must intervene. I pulled one of the mothers aside and informed her I would love to make a contribution. Assuming it was financial aid, she immediately informed me they couldn't take a check.

"I have something far better in mind than a check," I told her as yet another shopper sailed past the popcorn display. "I'll show you and your pep squad a surefire way to sell more popcorn."

Two weeks later, when their next fundraising event began, they were prepared. It was a Sunday, shortly before game time. Armed with an electric generator, since Wal-Mart said no to extension cords, the cheerleaders displayed a table with two microwaves, popping their fresh corn. The girls gave samples to everyone entering or leaving the store. The table also held several shaker-style toppings, including cheddar cheese, caramel, cinnamon spice, and vegetable medley. This slowed the traffic flow long enough for shoppers to purchase their favorite flavor.

The girls also stopped the crowd in their tracks when they gave a cheer of appreciation. At the end of the hour, the popcorn was gone.

Spending a little of their own capital in order to exceed their customers' expectations produced the best results in the school's popcorn sales history. Fran, one of the mothers, informed me that next time they will also offer mini water bottles printed with their insignia. Great job, Mustangs!

SENIOR'S CENTER

Whatever happened to full-service gas pumps? If you're old enough to remember full service, you know that society has slowly disconnected from providing great service, and this is an excellent example. These days, no one cares.

Or do they? Senior's Center does. They decided to listen to the population over age sixty-five. Okay, it was my idea, but the proprietors of this superlative business were inspired by my friend Gladys, who griped about having to pump her own gas. With arthritis in both hands, she was forced to rely on others to fill up her car. Her son, Philip, gladly assumed that duty when his mother was sixty-seven. In California, shoving the huge, plastic, EPA-enforced plastic nozzles into your tank is a challenge even for the young bucks.

An estimated thirty-three million people will be over the age of seventy in the next five years, and many will still drive. This may well be the scariest part of the equation.

Is this an opportunity to serve these elderly greats? I believe it is. Senior's Center is a full-service fueling station designed exclusively for the aging population. Philip Larsen and his wife, Sue, have an idea that could grow into a great franchise opportunity across the country someday. Imagine another place where you can receive respect for being mature in age. Styles of clothes come back. Why not full service?

The Larsens have also started serving fresh food at their station. When the customer pulls into the island for fuel, he can also place an order for food as well. A staff member delivers it right to their vehicle while the attendant finishes up with the service. This business model is so popular that when you drive by, you'll swear you are witnessing the return of odd/even gas because the line is so long.

YOUR BUSINESS AS A MINISTRY OPPORTUNITY

Your employees, or partners as I like to refer to them, are your business' lifeblood. I'm discovering this as we begin to open more stores. Whether your business employs two or two hundred, your goal should be to maintain your doctrine when you're absent and no one notices.

Given the current economic environment, there's plenty of talent available. How do you attract this abundant talent and keep them? One of my favorite Bible stories is the time when the Jewish hierarchy chastised Jesus for his unsavory associations and he explained that he entertained non-followers for the opportunity it presented to teach them about God's plan.

Interestingly, all but one of my staff entered the $5,000 Car Store already saved by Jesus Christ. Providing a community which allows growth toward Jesus Christ should be within your daily planner. It truly is a contagious momentum.

JUST STARTING OUT?

If you are still in the planning stages of your small business, one of my future books. *Thirty Ways to Win*, will help you. In it, I'll offer over thirty small business opportunities I believe to be surefire winners that the baby boom population will patronize over the coming years. We shouldn't dismiss the demographic promise of the gray wave.

The principles taught in this book are essential ingredients to success. Christian ethics is the divider that separates the average from the exceedingly beyond average. Make your faith the cornerstone for the management of your business, and success will abound. Don't forget to share this blessing with your brothers and sisters, for we are all equals.

THE TAKEAWAY: Mr. Failure, whose sole purpose is to produce business failures in this country, met with his three closest advisors one morning and contemplated ways to increase the rate of small business start-up failures. He asked them, "What can we say to these wannabe entrepreneurs who seek a run at success?"

His first advisor snatched a fat cigar from his mouth. "We can tell them that every great business strategy has already been thought of and that there's nothing new to discover."

"No," Mr. Failure said. "There's a new book in print that debunks that myth."

His second advisor typed meeting notes into his laptop. "We can tell them there is no such thing as failure. We'll artificially soften them with the notion that everyone succeeds at a new business the first time out. Being naïve, they'll be totally unprepared and step in front of that oncoming train."

"No," Mr. Failure said. "Some might actually do it and become successful by purchasing this new business playbook."

His third advisor glanced at his diamond-studded

wristwatch. "We can tell them there's no hurry. Don't worry about it; you have plenty of time. Go and play, enjoy your life. It's so short."

The vote was unanimous. Doing nothing, they concluded, was all it would take for many business owners to keep from discovering the difference between victory and failure.

HALFTIME

AN OPPORTUNITY TO TAKE INVENTORY

Oakland's Officer Greg Delbridge had the uncanny ability to arrive on crime scenes ahead of everyone else. This talent earned him the nickname "the Buzzard" after the high-flying bird who can spot fresh road-kill five miles away. This 1971 Rookie of the Year had a bright future; however, the events of the early hours of Tuesday, March 12, 1979, changed everything.

Under cover of darkness, two gunmen wearing ski masks robbed Crisco's Market at Twelfth and Broadway. A disabled stock clerk, who had been beaten repeatedly by the gunmen, activated the silent alarm. As the two robbers raced from the store, they encountered Officer Delbridge's squad car careening over the curb. It then crashed into the storefront's entrance.

The perpetrators aimed their sawed-off shotguns at the windshield as they barreled through the broken double-glass doors. Greg's reflexes told him just in time to duck for cover. Both robbers' weapons went off at once, spraying buckshot directly through the patrol car's windshield and scattering glass everywhere.

Moments later, Greg lifted his head from the wreckage, unsure whether he'd been hit and not knowing whether the robbers would finish their heinous crime and end his life as he sat there, vulnerable.

When no further shots came, Greg climbed from his pummeled vehicle, realizing that he had cheated death as surely as the two gunmen had burglarized the store.

> *"Halftime is an opportunity to adjust your direction before you win or lose the game."*

The Oakland Police Department gave Greg three months off with pay to recover from his traumatic ordeal. Greg refers to this as his halftime. He never forgot his high-school football coach's definition of halftime. In the locker room during a big Friday night game, he told the team, "Halftime is an opportunity to adjust your direction before you win or lose the game. It's a time to take inventory of where you've been and where you want to go."

Later that year, Officer Delbridge, "the Buzzard," returned to the force, and he had a different game plan. He liked the idea of living but knew the risks of his position. He figured he'd been spared for a reason. He would soon discover his true gift to the Kingdom.

Greg and I met after his routine call to the Metropolitan Yacht Club. A band of vigilante merchants had apprehended a would-be purse-snatcher and were holding him in the upstairs lounge. Officer Delbridge, passing through the club, smelled the aroma of Northern Italy wafting in from the downstairs kitchen, where my staff and I were dishing up a tricolored Italian lunch of tortellini pesto, fettuccine alfredo, and lasagna for the club members.

Officer Delbridge peered through the doorway and pointed his long finger at me. "I'll be back."

We all gazed at him, then at each other. Which of us was he coming back for?

About an hour later, he sat down to lunch with my staff and me. We bonded immediately. I was one month from closing escrow on the sale of the Culinarian and had burned myself to a crisp. Two and a half years of nonstop catering had plastered the stress onto my face, a look that Greg recognized instantly.

After everyone left, he stayed and talked to me for over three hours while he counseled me on life and what it meant to him. It took a near-death trauma to make him realize the reason he was spared: to pass on his experience to others. This subject matter could never be taught in a textbook; the teacher must live it before he can teach it.

"The Buzzard" became the California's leading expert on playing out stressful behavior, specializing in a newly created department named "Halftime Thinking." Law enforcement and high-ranking politicians use this curriculum to asses the risks before they pursue new endeavors.

Greg soon taught me two of his all-time favorite plays, which he uses to coach his team. He believes that complacency causes us to overlook important items by numbing the mind and preventing clear thinking. The solution is to take a personal halftime and discover your "refresh button." This is the only way to overcome the numbing sensation life gives to you. Then you can pursue victory as a focused individual.

CREATE YOUR OWN HALFTIME

We all have an inner compass that leads us to think about happiness, peace, or a comfort zone. Where's yours? This is where you need to gravitate when you feel absent from the world in which you reside. Unfortunately, some people escape to drugs, alcohol, gambling, or some other destructive avenue. Arriving at our peaceful place while in our right mind is the key.

I have a friend who can't decide whether he's still a Bernalillo county sheriff or a car dealer. His halftime therapy is a fishing trip on the San Juan River in northern New Mexico with two buddies. He takes a trip about every three months, and before he leaves, he develops an I-don't-care attitude and makes poor business decisions. When he comes back, he's a new person, ready to dive into work again.

The only problem is the high-risk time between trips. During those weeks, he exercises poor judgment and suffers from stress and anxiety. As a result of my teaching, he now visits this comfort zone daily, which improves both his mental state and his business sense.

My comfort zone is in conversation with the Trinity. Before I begin my day, I always visit with the Father, Son and Holy Spirit. I leave home knowing that my inventory belongs to God. On Wednesdays, I'm out the door at 4:30 in the morning so I can catch a plane to purchase vehicles out of state. If I forgo my time with God on those days, it sometimes leaves me off my game. Because I have to be at my peak performance, I incorporate prayer therapy into my schedule to ward off failure and achieve victory.

AVOID THE COMPLACENCY TRAP

The problem for most people is that their refresh buttons are in places they can't reach during the daily grind. I recommend that you take pictures of those places, people, or events and plaster them near your desk or work area. That way, your comfort zone is always within reach.

Greg told me his refresh button is everywhere he looks. And he's not joking. Both his boys, Greg Jr. and Garret, played sports since they were old enough to say the word. Inspired by the book *The Training of a Tiger* by Earl Woods, Greg set out to teach his boys that sports will instill the character they need in order to achieve greatness.

When the boys were ten, Greg began photographing every sporting event they competed in. Garret, who proudly displays his UCLA Bruin uniform and Greg Jr., who wears

Stanford cardinal, are plastered onto every wall, including the headliner of Greg's BMW.

"This concept works like magic," Greg said.

And he's right. I've used this technique for several years, and it's amazing. It reminds me that victory in my business is not an option; it's a reality. In my living room hangs a large framed photo of my first dumpy Central Avenue location that still sits vacant today. It's properly titled, "The $5,000 Car Store, 2000."

Ironically, it's down the street from the lot where Bill Gates and Paul Allan initially set up their Microsoft company in 1976. The world is fortunate that they didn't allow complacency to rob them of their creativity. A halftime technique (a picture of Bill standing in front of their dilapidated building with a "for-lease" sign in the window) demonstrates how they visualized greater potential and moved their company back to Bellevue, Washington, on January 1, 1979.

CHAPTER 9

IT'S THE ENTIRE TEAM

THE DEFENSIVE LINE-UP: My business is not growing. The economy is terrible and I have stagnated. I don't think I can wait for a recovery to arrive.

OFFENSIVE STRATEGY: A recession is not an acceptable argument for business stagnation. Instead, blame your lack of ministry to the team. Your business is all about living relationships. If your team members aren't fed, they will die. The trajectory to survival and growth is simple: if you're not constantly raising the bar for the people who support you (your team), failure will result. Begin your service to them and watch success flourish within your company.

Ronald Reagan's aide recalled an incident that occurred in the spring of 1981 while the president was recovering from the bullet wound he sustained during the assassination attempt. Mother Theresa, the saintly nun who ministered to the poorest and the dying in Calcutta, visited the president shortly after the shooting.

"You have suffered the passion of the cross," she told him. "Surely God has spared you for a reason."

The shaken president agreed. "He spared me so that I can devote the rest of my days to serving him."

Through many hours of study and research, I had gotten to know the president pretty well. His deep faith, prior to this tragic event, was always his number one conviction, even higher in his priorities than his relationship with his wife, Nancy. The service to God of which he spoke was the dismantling of Communism and the threat it posed to America and the world.

On a very humid night on August 23, 1984, in Dallas, Texas, Ronald Reagan served the country in a way that I believe would make any American proud. Politics aside, at his reelection convention, Mr. Reagan said, "America, you ain't seen nothing yet."

From the moment he took office, he made it clear that he believed America stood for a great idea, the Soviet Union a bad one. Continually underestimated, he proved his skeptics wrong on several occasions.

My friends, this is the power of faith through service that only God can bring about. As Margaret Thatcher put it, "Ronald Reagan won the Cold War without firing a shot."

Pretty remarkable for a man who most believed was a B-rated actor, renegade cowboy from California, and incapable of running a country, let alone changing the world. I illustrate Mr. Reagan here because of his humble and modest upbringing and how he chose to serve as a result of it. He went to serve in the vineyard at age 69 and made history.

The crash and burn most successful people experience is a direct result of sacrificing humility for fame. It's that simple. We read countless examples every day. This is without a doubt the biggest mistake we mortals make, and it's manufactured into us.

I love watching the lanes at the auctions where I purchase my vehicles. I can always tell when a high-profile vehicle enters the lane just before the auctioneer places it for sale. This Tuesday night, it's a "bright red" 2009 Chevy Camaro rolling forward. Behind it, they swarm like bees: ten to twenty dealers, their handheld electronic devices instructing them how to bid. Like salmon chasing a shiny lure, they follow behind, mesmerized. The auctioneer heightens the tension by drumming up the vehicle and stopping the momentum just long enough to capture all who wish to participate in this bidding frenzy.

I can guarantee you, the vehicle sold for more than their Blackberries instructed: twenty-two thousand dollars.

"Who cares?" grunts the new owner. "Look, everyone; I'm the guy who bought it."

You can view this pride-based, too-pricey purchase on his Web site beginning tonight. Unfortunately for them, he'll find customers who can't live without this high-end transportation. Incidentally, the $5,000 Car Store has no Web site. We're too busy. Who needs one? God has blessed me with the challenges of servicing my customers' expectations through ministry. This consumes every minute of my time, and we set sales records both monthly and yearly.

The next vehicle driving through the auction lane is a light hail-damaged 2002 Ford Explorer with little dealer interest. That's the one I'll purchase, and it's the one my customers are thankful for yet proud to drive. Guess what? I don't need a handheld device or *Kelly Blue Book* to tell me what my customers will pay for it.

Let's change this by providing humility to our team, beginning with the people who put forth effort every day on your company's behalf. It starts with you, the CEO. In order to pull this off, you'll have to remember that it's not about you; it's about putting others first and yourself last.

Serving others is the cornerstone of successful humility. Seek ways to praise and lift up these wonderful people, for without them you have nothing.

> *"Serving others is the cornerstone of successful humility."*

I begin my day by dreaming of ways to bring out my staff's best attributes. For example, I'll select one person to zoom in on every couple of days. Perhaps I'll prepare Harold's favorite lunch, BBQ pork sandwiches. This lets everyone know this is Harold's day.

Harold runs our paint and body shop and consistently

produces one vehicle per day. He is so proud to bring his latest work to the dealership. He has a place in the back to park them where no sticky fingers can find them before they dry.

On his day, I park his shiny, freshly painted vehicle in front of the dealership. I prop a "Just Painted" sign nearby for everyone to see. I make it a point to let everyone, including customers, know how proud we are of his work. Is there a difference in Harold's attitude this day? Yes, there is.

April is the general manager of our first car store. Her four years of dedicated service have been instrumental to the growth of this company. Constantly searching for ways to show my appreciation, I came up with this idea.

Chapter 5, "Feed Your Team," was started for her. Prior to our healthy lunchtime meal program, she indulged herself in any fast food available. Since she was slightly overweight and self-conscious about it, I introduced a healthier alternative, just for her. Attempting to serve only one person, we ended up changing the lives of many in the process. Her weight loss has restored confidence in her that is beautiful to witness every day.

Obviously, the service you provide your customers is crucial to your survival too. A current data base of all your contacts is an essential tool. Here's one way to reach all of them with one whack. Last year's $5,000 Car Store's Christmas card offered a special gift: a free oil change and vehicle inspection at one of our shops. A nice gesture, but what meant more than the material gift was the kind and thoughtful message inside. "I've never seen anything like this from a business before," Julie Sanchez said in an Internet review.

Dear Valued Customer of the $5,000 Car Store,

If we don't know your first name, your children's names, what vehicle you purchased, and where you work, then shame on us for not paying closer attention to the details that matter most.

This ministry expands through you and your loyalty, not us, and we thank you. We know that more than eleven hundred New Mexico dealers would love to sell you a vehicle. When you chose us, we hoped first to establish a relationship that would give you the confidence and trust to tell your friends and relatives about us.

If you should ever need anything, my staff and partners are here to help. On behalf of our entire organization, thank you and God bless, and have a very Merry Christmas and Happy New Year.

Blessings, Steve

Christmas cards provide a great opportunity to reach out once a year and show appreciation to your customers. Another dealer once told me, "There's no point in building a relationship with someone who buys a car. I don't want the headache of having to deal with them coming back asking for more." However, for any business, not servicing what you sell is nothing else than selfishness and greed. This policy is destined to fail. People talk to one another. Let them say great things about your company. If you should Google "5000 Car Store," you'll see exactly what I'm talking about.

PRACTICING HUMILITY

Practicing humility does not mean that we view everyone else as superior, better, or more talented. Rather, humble love sees others as worthy of preferential treatment. That is exactly how I perceive my customers and employees. This precise formula sets our dealership apart from its competitors. It begins with a belief and it resonates far beyond what is otherwise possible.

Business can sometimes be overwhelming: sole proprietor, Steve Henry; owner-operator, Steve Henry; author, Steve Henry; real estate investor, Steve Henry. I'm here to see Steve. Sign here, Steve. Two calls holding for Steve.

I once read that if you see your name in print or hear your name often, your head will swell. In this chapter, I hope to inject enough safeguards so this potentially dangerous outcome doesn't occur and your focus can remain strictly on serving others, not yourself.

The best definition of humility I've ever seen came from the *Christian Leadership Journal*, January 1, 1984: "Humility is not denying the power you have but admitting that the power comes through you and not from you. If you deny the power you've been given, you lie. If you have a fine voice, to depreciate it is to show a lack of appreciation for it. If you've been given a talent for making money (and I believe it is a talent), then use it and be the trustee of it. If your talent is administration, then help things to happen. I don't believe that God is giving any talent for irresponsibility, and that is what we are showing when we fail to recognize, appreciate, and use the talent we have been given."

It's easy to fall prey to the notion that your success is due to something you have done. This is a difficult challenge to overcome. From birth, we're wired to use tantrums to demand the things we desire, thus feeding the notion that it's all about us and our needs. Nothing could be further from "It's the Entire Team" doctrine.

In order to keep my humble perspective, I use safeguards and keep myself aligned. I highly suggest you search your business for areas of humility that will keep you focused on serving others. When prideful tendencies come like that roaring lion Peter warns us about, insert barriers to remind yourself to retreat immediately. Here are a few of mine, which I practice daily.

I COULD DRIVE ANY VEHICLE I WISH

I choose to drive whatever takes me back and forth to work. You'll never see me in a personal vehicle that you wouldn't find on the front line of my stores.

I COULD WEAR BETTER CLOTHING

If you happened by my store and asked for Steve, you wouldn't be able to tell who Steve was by looking at what I'm wearing. I wear exactly what my customers or employees would on any given day.

RANKED IN THE TOP TEN ON VOLUME
AT AUCTION; SO WHAT?

You'll never see me parked in the "Reserved for Special Dealers" space or hobnobbing with the big guns of the auction house. Between my purchases, I prefer to chat with the rank and file rather than the management or big-name dealers. Ask any auction employee where he goes to purchase his vehicles. One dealer sells to more auction employees than the rest. You guessed it: the $5,000 Car Store. I treat them as though I'm invading their space, respectful of the job they do, as opposed to the attitude that they should serve me because I'm a dealer.

MY OFFICE COULD BE THE BIGGEST AND BEST

Not only would you not be able to identify who the owner is by what he drives or wears, but where he sits would also be a mystery. My desk is the same as everyone else's. Is yours?

HUMBLE PRINCIPLES DICTATE SUCCESS

When an employee or customer raises an issue of concern, I always resolve it by using what the authors of the New Testament would prescribe. Christian leadership principles are exactly what's missing in today's business climate. Customers who are tired of mistrust, disrespect, and condescending attitudes will migrate to our side over time. Be constantly on patrol for service opportunities.

It's difficult—putting others first, serving, tolerating, and sacrificing—but it's worth it. We continue to contract Ms. Yazzie without grimacing, even when Junior's diapers filled up, emptying out the entire lobby one busy Friday afternoon, while the mom did nothing about it. Now that's service! Our second store, which opened last summer, blasted off the charts without any advertising because of the humble principles we exhibit daily in our first store.

The Playbook for Small Businesses will assist you in this area. Humility is more important than staffing your company with the brightest minds and the most qualified applicants. A competitor recently ran an advertisement seeking salespeople for his dealership. It read, "Local dealer seeking qualified, experienced salespeople for commission and bonuses. Minimum three years' experience required."

Have you ever driven into a car dealership and seen at least twenty of these salespeople waiting for your vehicle to come to a complete stop? Did you know that 52 percent of people who come "just looking" end up succumbing to the purchase of a car because of the relentless pressure these salespeople apply? If you're lucky enough to get away and take time to think your purchase through, then the follow-up phone calls you'll receive over the next week will surely lead to capitulation.

I believe there is a place for commission sales, but not at my business. If we're all aware of the reputation that follows these high-pressure tactics, why on earth do we allow that stench in our business? In a ministry-led business, your customers pressure you for the sale they wish to execute. Is this possible? Of course it is, if you receive and understand the laborer's story.

We have never hired a commissioned salesperson and employ only people who understand and accept our way of treating our customers. By offering a ministry style of service and a product that we stand behind, we exceed our customers' expectations, which produces recession-proof, record sales.

THE TAKEAWAY: How do you prepare to use humble tactics to manage a company? Simply put everyone first and yourself last. Here is a New Testament scripture I've modified to illustrate how this may be possible:

For the act of humility is like a landowner who went out early in the morning to hire men to work in his vineyard. He agreed to pay them a denarius, for the day (in those days about twenty cents, a day's wages) and sent them into his vineyard.

About the third hour he went out and saw others standing in the marketplace doing nothing. He told them, "You also go and work in my vineyard, and I will pay you whatever is right." So they went.

He went out again about the sixth hour and the ninth hour and did the same thing. About the eleventh hour, he went out and found still others standing around. He asked them, "Why have you been standing here all day long, doing nothing?"

"Because no one has hired us," they answered. He said to them, "You also go and work in my vineyard."

When evening came, the owner of the vineyard said to his foreman, "Call the workers and pay them their wages, beginning with the last ones hired and going on to the first."

The workers who were hired about the eleventh hour came, and each received a denarius. So, when those came who were hired first, they expected to receive more. But each one of them also received a denarius. When they received it, they began to grumble against the landowner. "These men who were hired last worked only one hour," they said, "and you have made them equal to us who have borne the burden of the work and the heat of the day."

But he answered one of them, "Friend, I am not being unfair to you. Didn't you agree to work for a denarius? Take your pay and go. I want to give the man who was hired last the same as I gave you. Don't I have the right to do what I want with my own money? Or are you envious because I am generous?"

I would like to introduce to you the cast in this story.

> **The Landowner:** The act of humility and its reward for the giving of service to others

> **The Vineyard:** Your ministry-led business (the $5,000 Car Store)

> **The Workday:** The here and now

> **The Workers:** Those who have decided to spend the rest of their lives serving others

The Work Hours: The different ages that one decides to serve

The Lesson: It doesn't matter when you decide to serve humbly, just so you do it. The reward is the same, always open to all, even until the last hour. Those who are called early have no "bragging rights" over those who come later.

The Benefits: Your customers will experience the passion, commitment, and concern you transmit. Upon receiving them, they will be reluctant to return to your competitor.

CHAPTER 10

LOVE YOUR POSITION

THE DEFENSIVE LINE-UP: Your close friends and family members constantly remind you, "You're so good at this; it comes naturally to you." "Start a business—you'll make lots of money."

OFFENSIVE STRATEGY: Seven out of ten initial start-ups will vanish before their first year has ended. Learn to recognize and react to your gifted energy. Reject all opportunities that someone else with biased motivations has selected for you. A successful business emerges from within. Save yourself from—yourself.

On May 11, 1996, ValuJet Airline flight 592, a DC-9 with a flight plan departing Miami en route to Atlanta, took off at 2:04 p.m. The jet began a normal climb.

However, at 2:10 p.m., the flight crew noted an electrical problem. Seconds later, an attendant blasted into the cockpit. "Fire in the cabin!"

Passengers' shouts of "Fire! Fire!" were recorded on the plane's voice recorder when the cockpit door was opened.

The crew immediately radioed air traffic control and asked to return to Miami due to smoke in the cockpit and cabin. Captain Candi Kubeck and First Officer Richard Hazen were given instructions to return to the airport. One minute later, the first officer requested the nearest airport.

Flight 592 disappeared from radar at 2:14 p.m. It crashed in Browns Farm Wildlife Management Area in the Everglades, a few miles west of Miami, at speeds in excess of 500 miles per hour. All 105 passengers and five flight crew members aboard were killed. The DC-9 shattered on impact with the bedrock, leaving very few large portions of the plane intact.

At the time, I was an investment advisor as a hobby. Thirty minutes before the stock market opened on the Monday morning following this tragic Saturday afternoon crash, my phone rang. It was Jerry Pineal from Tallahassee. "It's down over 25 percent! Should I sell ValuJet? You told me this was a safe and wise investment. Thanks a lot, Steve!"

This was just one of several hundred phone calls I received regarding the fallout from this dire event. In my newsletter the month prior to the accident, I recommended

ValuJet to my subscribers at twelve dollars a share, up 20 percent. Since its 1994 initial public offering (IPO), which is the first public sale of stock by a new company, ValuJet's share price had skyrocketed over 100 percent.

The news coverage throughout the weekend inspired negative press. Speculation about the cause of the crash swirled from transportation of illegally marked chemicals to missing mechanics to the hordes of temporary employees and subcontractors that earned ValuJet the nickname "the virtual airline." Who was responsible?

It was devastating. Soon after the FAA and the National Transportation Safety Board began their investigations, it became apparent that this once high-flying discount airline's future was in danger.

Four years prior to the ValuJet tragedy, Snapple Beverage from Valley Stream, New York, was a brand- new idea the Phoenix Metro market snatched up. As a result of an explosive retail distribution launch, you could now buy bottled, high-quality iced tea in a plethora of inviting flavors. All the consumers I spoke with agreed: Snapple answered their requests. This flavored iced tea would have a profound impact on the beverage industry around the world.

At its IPO in December 1992, shares sold for twenty dollars. The price ratcheted to over fifty dollars by the spring of 1993. I recommended this company's stock, and everyone who purchased it realized huge profits. The stock continued to outperform, even after the "copycats" (Lipton and Pepsi) climbed on board with their own versions.

The Breathe Right nasal strip story was another grand

slam I recommended to my clients at eight dollars a share. A non-medicated nasal strip, placed across a man's nose so his wife can sleep at night, resulted in saving hundreds of marriages from IWS (irritable wife syndrome). It was a no-brainer.

The company gained national notoriety in late October 1994. On Monday Night Football, Super Bowl MVP wide receiver Jerry Rice wore a Breathe Right strip across his nose during the game. That night, he happened to have one of his best performances of the season.

"They really do work," he said. The stock vaulted over 200 percent to thirty-eight dollars as a publicly traded company the next year.

Since I had predicted these fabulous stock trends, I thought that trading was the niche for me. I became convinced after I spoke to a prominent Wall Street hedge fund manager, Xavier Blythe. He said, "You are blessed with an uncanny ability to ferret out these small upstarts with huge potential. I've never seen anyone with such consistent victories."

Several of my friends also benefited from my investment advice. Since I had the gift of discovering companies on the cutting edge of an earnings upside explosion due to a new successful product or service launch, they thought I should share the wealth. They begged me to publish a newsletter, and I did.

With annualized returns of over 110 percent, the Steve Henry News Letter amassed subscribers by the hundreds. I advertised in the Investors Business Daily every other

Friday, and the calls my headquarters generated were unbe-lievable. For only sixty-five dollars a year, you could receive excellent recommendations on stocks about to skyrocket in price. I circulated this twelve-page publication every six weeks throughout the United States and Canada.

> *"I wasn't in love with this business... I didn't listen to my heart"*

The timing couldn't have been better. Brokerage houses were dropping their fees, and online trading was here to stay. If you didn't like my stock picks, every barber in the city had one of his own. The problem was, while I liked developing and circulating my newsletter, I didn't love it.

This, my friends, is why at the end of that fateful Monday; I decided my stock advisory newsletter was finished. After ValuJet flight 592 and its effects on people's lives, I no longer felt good about offering investment advice.

I knew deep down that I wasn't in love with this business relationship, but I didn't listen to my heart. Until now, no one has known why my publication ended. Most investment gurus get it wrong for a living and have no remorse, but I couldn't bear the thought of someone losing money or sleep on my watch.

However, with several hundred paid subscriptions, I had to maintain my composure and continue to write great advice for the rest of the year.

This is how my Sacramento neighbor, John Ramsey, felt after his barbeque restaurant closed its doors. He told me, "I liked the idea, but I felt coerced into a relationship I wasn't in love with."

I strongly encourage you to heed this valuable lesson. I hope that when your friends, family, and colleagues encourage you to pursue their lovely dream, you will first make sure it's your dream. If you're not in love with the idea, its outcome will eventually be recorded as a failure in the books of business history. Sounds just like a personal relationship, doesn't it?

Are You in Love?

This chapter will help you to confirm in your heart, without trepidation, that you should not launch your raft into the rushing white waters and establish a business relationship before knowing that you can swim. Of course, you've already determined that your gifted energy has allowed you this opportunity. You've selected some favorite playbook ideas to implement.

But are you in love with the idea? Is it your heartfelt passion? Are you willing to commit your heart, soul, mind, and strength? I have composed a simple exercise to assist you with these questions. Here are eight of my daily business game-day strategies that confirm my love of the business relationship for the team on which I play. I'm aware that if I can't commit to these, I can't engage myself to victory.

HOW I KNOW I'M IN THE RIGHT GAME

Choose any business—there's going to be a single day within a week or a month that we'll call game day. It's the most important day. I don't know of a single business that doesn't have one day in which it needs to be on top, or else the rest of the week or month will suffer as a result. There's a saying in the car business that the profit is realized, not when the vehicle sells to the customer, but when the dealer purchases it. This is a true statement. So my game day is once a week, every Thursday. It begins with a visit to the only vehicle auction in my state.

I compete for that great purchase alongside fifty other dealers interested in the same inventory as I am. If I'm lucky, there might be thirty vehicles that I will want to purchase. This is where my challenge begins. Buying for two stores, I need to purchase about twenty vehicles per week.

As you can see, the odds are against me. The logical answer is to pay the highest price and be done with it. But that's not how I will stay in business and claim victory. The failure rate in this business is a staggering 80 percent within the first five years. One obvious reason is overpaying. Any idiot can raise his hand to the bitter end and walk away victorious but not stay in business.

Here's how you'll know you're in the right game. Proceed with a "throttle up" mindset. Stacked against me are the odds of purchasing the inventory I require. I prevail, not sometimes, but almost all the time.

Here's how I do it. I begin my mental preparations the

night before. I allow no instability, for on game day I must be victorious. The arena I play in is outside. I'm challenged with adverse weather conditions, restrooms that maintain a line of at least five minutes (got to really watch what you eat the night before) and a limited time—one hour—in which to test-drive all my potential purchases on a track that allows for a top speed of only forty miles per hour.

Focusing on the outcome, I'm the first one to arrive the morning of game day. I preview the inventory I'll purchase, listening one by one for any irregularities in the motor and transmission. Then I carefully inspect each vehicle I plan to purchase.

I do this with the utmost enthusiasm, conviction, and excitement, knowing what is at stake. There isn't anything else I'd rather be doing on this fifteen-degree morning. When I return exhausted to the dealership, about 2 p.m., I begin strategizing how to mobilize the purchases to their proper places for front-line readiness. If on your game day you don't play with this type of intensity, perhaps you're in the wrong game.

LOVE-DRIVEN PASSION
SHALL CONQUER ALL OBSTACLES

The stock market opens conveniently on Eastern Time, making the hours of operation on the West Coast very early. It shouldn't matter what time of day your passion requires your attention. I never missed a premarket opening; it was that important. I did not love the phone calls or e-mails I'd receive at that hour, asking me investment questions. I'd much prefer them to read my newsletter. (Warning #1)

Ronnie has his own roofing company in Phoenix, Arizona. From late May through September, the afternoon rooftop temperatures can climb to over 125 degrees.

His entire staff clocks in eight hours before noon every day during the summer months. He always has a light breakfast waiting for his employees and all the delivery drivers at their 3:30 a.m. designated rendezvous spot. (See Chapter 5: "Feed the Team." Way to go, Ronnie!)

I'm not sure what time he starts his day, or should I say night? His game day is Friday. This is when the general contracting foreman drops by each job site to inspect the week's work. The most productive team is awarded the best schedule, which generates the largest profits for the team. They truly "love their position."

NEVER, EVER BE LATE

It's not okay for you to retaliate against the rest of the world for its tardiness. Think of your punctuality as an expression of your passion to win. Maybe your employees and clients aren't believers yet, but perhaps someday they will see the light. Discipline yourself and set the example.

In my case, early constitutes victory. I love to watch a competitor pay top dollar for a vehicle with a slipping transmission because he didn't arrive early to preview his potential mistakes. People are watching. This is the easiest area in which to show something different at work in your life. It begins with you being not on time, but early every day.

DON'T FEAR SUCCESS

Since you know that God's blessing is upon you, the only thing you have to fear is—nothing! Two distinct things will occur as you launch out.

First will come euphoria over the notion that your business plan has great potential. My phone didn't stop ringing on those super Fridays. I followed my scripted speech, collected a credit card number, and mailed out the recent copy of the newsletter. I had a gigantic map of the United States and Canada, and I'd stick a pin in each town in which I had a subscriber. This ten-by-six-foot map hung in my fourteen-foot work station, between two computers. At first glance, things couldn't have looked better.

As the pins filled the map, the second phase started. I realized the magnitude of my responsibility. It was intimidating to look at that map and consider how many people counted on me to deliver stellar results. The warm, fuzzy love feelings quickly turned to fear and anxiety. (Warning #2)

I HAD BETTER HAVE MY GAME FACE ON

Believers in a successful business plan have a spring to their step. One way we can portray this exuberance is to present ourselves consistently radiating the passion we share for our business. This begins with our customers and their satisfaction. Never forget; without them there's no relationship

THE PLAYBOOK *for* SMALL BUSINESSES

in which to love. Do they see you as a champion who loves what he does?

ALWAYS ASK,
"WHAT CAN WE IMPROVE ON TODAY?"

Not a day goes by when I don't see opportunities to improve upon business, using *Playbook* principles. Don't get caught up in the "if it isn't broken, don't fix it" attitude. It will eventually result in failure.

Just ask the makers of Clearly Canadian. They launched an alternative beverage (which was excellent) in the late 1980s and immediately witnessed customer acceptance. But they never introduced a diet drink or any additional flavors to their product line. Year after year, the company relied on the never-changing, boring flavors to float their flagship.

When was the last time you saw their product on the beverage shelf? They failed because of their lack of continual integration into their market. Snapple saw this as an opportunity and constantly changed their mix of flavors. Soon they became the new alternative-beverage maker.

We can bring this same concept to the small business. Recently, I was assisting in getting some emissions inspections done for our cars and was vehicle number four in line. Emissions inspection is an annual obligation in many cities, and you have to get it done before you can register your vehicle. Most people think it's a complete waste of time. They postpone the inspection until the last minute on the last day before expiration. All our vehicles undergo this process before we park them in the front line.

That day, the ninety-plus degree temperatures made it uncomfortable for many patrons without air conditioning. At the time, I didn't know the owner, Rudy. But I suggested that he have someone come to the car windows and serve a cold drink, an assortment of wrapped candy, granola bars, or fresh fruit while the customers wait.

Less than a week later, Juan told me that Rudy had his seventeen-year-old daughter in uniform with a service tray in her hand, rotating between cars, offering small drinks and snacks to every vehicle waiting in line. Gwen, his service tech inside the booth, told Juan, "Our customers love it and approach the service area in much better moods."

Interestingly, the line of cars waiting for their inspection, which used to average four vehicles, now runs seven and eight. Their competitor down the street is furious! And none of the customers seem to mind the ten-minute wait.

WHO CAN WE HELP TODAY?

The letter I received from Suzanne Bluehouse revealed a disgruntled customer. The 2000 Chevy Blazer she'd purchased from me four months prior had transmission issues. Replacing the transmission would cost her over three thousand dollars.

I'd never received a piece of mail like this before. I responded to her positively, and after several meetings, I agreed to replace her transmission. On the test drive to check out the new transmission, the engine made a loud ticking noise at seventy miles per hour and began to spew oil everywhere. When the vehicle came to a stop along Interstate 40, it was clear the motor was blown.

Reluctantly, with some help, I replaced her motor too. Never overlook an opportunity to help someone in need, even if it costs you more than you ever intended to spend. Suzanne called me a couple weeks later and invited me to a private dinner party where I had the pleasure of meeting our city's three-term mayor, Marty Chavez, and several state officials. We had a wonderful discussion about a very successful small business with a *Playbook* manual that's soon to be released to the public.

YOU CAN'T WAIT FOR AN OPPORTUNITY
TO TALK ABOUT YOUR BUSINESS

You know you're in love with your business when you convey your progress and passion at every opportunity. From the first few sentences, I can determine if someone loves what she does. She exudes confidence without negativity, guided by the Spirit, knowing she is in charge of her company's future.

THE TAKEAWAY: How do you decide which position you ought to play and when? You'll know in your heart when you "throttle up." Pursuing your dreams and becoming the very best you can be was best described by the late Lieutenant Colonel Dick Scobee: "When you find something you really like to do, and you're willing to risk the consequences, you probably ought to do it."

This was a man who knew the risks and took one for the team. He knew exactly what he wanted to do and did it.

Before you decide whether starting your own business is the right decision, listen to a true hero's last words—one minute after *Challenger's* launch.

CAPCOM's Richard Covey, Challenger Houston: "You are go at throttle up."

Dick Scobee: "Roger, Houston, *throttle up*"

CHAPTER 11

THE CHAMPION WITHIN

THE DEFENSIVE LINE-UP: The thought of quitting my day job and becoming my own boss intrigues me. But every great idea has already been created and capitalized on. I'll stay here in my cubicle and wait for an opportunity to come to me. There's no point in disrupting what I have.

OFFENSIVE STRATEGY: You were not created merely to exist. There's a championship game inside you. Deciding to start your own business is a multistep process. Having faith and realizing you have championship tendencies are prerequisites to managing this journey successfully.

In 1981, with the country mired in a deep recession, starting a small business made about as much sense as selling wood stoves in Phoenix in mid-July. Having graduated with top honors from culinary school, I briefly accepted a position as head chef with a prominent Berkeley restaurant. I quickly discovered that my champion within was leading me to start my own business. I would later see my faith grow stronger as long as I remained on his superhighway and not Steve's Parkway. Are you following his superhighway?

Thus with a whopping four hundred dollars, the Culinarian Catering Company was born. I found a dilapidated yacht club in Jack London Square with a perfect location, nestled alongside the Oakland Marina with its own docking facilities and a waterfront view to die for. It had a commercial kitchen and full bar, a seating capacity of one hundred and fifty, and a membership of four hundred wannabe sailors.

The membership met every Friday, so I crafted a long-term lease in which I agreed to cater their lunches at a discounted price in return for free rent and use of their facility. With the economy on its knees, these prideful boat enthusiasts rarely used their club. It sat empty except for one annual function and the occasional business meeting or wedding of a member. The majority of the time, it worked out perfectly for my catered events. Within two years, I had accumulated the business of fourteen groups on a weekly basis, including Rotary, Kiwanis, Exchange, and Lyons clubs for their luncheon meetings.

The Culinarian's staff included my friend Mike Gallarda,

the artist, who was also creative in the kitchen. He and I brainstormed centerpiece themes for our catered events. For example, we catered a surprise seventy-fifth birthday party for Mr. Saunders. His wife, Ellen, told me he was an avid chess player and that all six of his grandchildren played like pros.

So Mike constructed a regulation-size chessboard out of orange and white cheese squares cut two inches thick. He then carved detailed chessmen from carrots and turnips, matching the board's colors. We displayed it as a chess game in progress, one move to checkmate.

When Mr. Saunders saw this, his face said it all. With tears running down both cheeks, he hugged me like a teddy bear. His guests were astonished too.

For Matt and Kathy's wedding, we found the biggest watermelon I've ever seen—forty-two pounds and thirty-four inches long. Mike carved it into a huge basket and filled it with fresh seasonal fruit. Then he perched this melon eight inches above a six-foot mirror with the bride and groom's names carved backward underneath the melon, completely out of sight. When the guests came to scoop out the fruit, reflecting back from the mirror image were the words, "Congratulations, Matt and Kathy Wagner."

The bride and groom stood by, watching their wedding guests view the surprise. Their comments to one another were the confirmation we anxiously awaited. We had exceeded their expectations. I can't stress how important this is. This will separate the champions from the failures.

During my culinary education, I practiced some theatrics

in my cooking labs. I discovered that providing great food and great ambiance was only part of the memorable dining entertainment experience. Exceeding your customer's expectations will always keep them talking.

> *"Exceeding your customer's expectations will always keep them talking."*

Unfortunately, this subject never appeared in our curriculum. That didn't stop me from juggling fruits, vegetables, knifes, skillets—anything I could throw in the air and catch. I received endless scolding from those staunch executive chefs who oversaw our labs.

Imagine my exuberance when Benihana's announced the opening of a new restaurant in sleepy old Concord, California, less than two miles from the Diablo Valley Junior College campus. Benihana's style of food is called "Teppanyaki."

Eating there is "equal parts restaurant, magic show, and performance art," said David Rockwell, the founder of the Rockwell Group, a Manhattan architecture firm that has designed more than seventy-five restaurants. Normally, you would find these restaurants only in markets like their first location at West 56th Street in Manhattan, Japantown in San Francisco, or Honolulu.

For days, I agonized over this opportunity. Should I apply for a position as an entertainer there? Would they be interested in someone so young? I finally made my decision.

On interview day, the line of kitchen personnel seeking

employment was at least a quarter of a mile long with a wait time of three hours to get an application. The interview would come later. As I peered around at the crowd, I saw that I was the youngest person in the line.

I managed to get a reservation for an interview the next day. A friend of mine, an insider, let me know what to expect if I should be lucky enough to speak to a chef. At my interview, the routine, food-related questions led to the big one I was anticipating. "Can you perform in front of a crowd of patrons while cooking their meal?"

"Yes! I can juggle knives, talk, and slice while preparing their requests."

Several days later, I received a phone call from one of the chefs in charge of hiring. He scheduled me for an audition the next day at 4 pm. This is how much emphasis Benihana's places on the chef's skill as an entertainer.

They gave us three hours to get acquainted with their system before our audition. Jazuko, the executive chef, gave us a demonstration of his act and told us what he expected from the four of us.

"Do you desire chicken fried rice with your lobster?" Jazuko speared a partially cooked chicken breast, and with razor-sharp knives in both hands, he literally shredded the breast into tiny pieces without the chicken ever touching the hot surface until he allowed it. He grabbed a scoop of steamed rice and some assorted vegetables. Then he cracked two eggs, which he scrambled with one hand, and with his spatula he formed a heart on the flat, steel grill. As the grand finale, this heart-shaped fried rice sculpture began beating right in front of us as it cooked. It was the most incredible theatrical display of food I'd ever seen.

Unable to get Chef Jazuko's performance out of my mind, I began to question my champion within. Have you, too, ever been outdone? Come up short? I believe we all have something to share on this topic. One of my biggest failures was attempting to become a pilot. In Albuquerque, the wind blows two hundred and fifty days a year with gusts up to forty miles per hour. Landing a Cessna 172 with these crosswinds seemed like a miracle to me, but to others, it's second nature. After nearly three times the normal training hours for this assignment, it became obvious to my instructor that I was never going to get it. We ended the lessons before someone got hurt. Still, the feeling of letdown is difficult to shake. This is God allowing you time to experiment, but through faith, he will steer you back to your rightful place. There's a great reason I didn't become a pilot, thanks to God.

At Benihana's, I was expected to perform my audition in front of a table of eight, communal style. The recently hired wait staff played the part of patrons ready to order from the performing chef.

The lights dimmed, the music began to play softly in the background, and the audience applauded as I made my way to the table. After a brief introduction and a bow, I now had three minutes to prove why I should be an entertainer at Benihana's.

I thought my performance went well. I used the dazzling knife-juggling act as my opener, playing on the crowd's sympathy in hopes I wouldn't stab myself.

My audition wasn't enough to convince the executives, for I never received a call-back. Feeling bummed, I later discovered that he had something better planned for me, as long as I kept my faith.

Next to selling my business for a staggering profit, the most memorable event of my career as CEO of the Culinarian would come in the summer of 1982. Excitement radiated throughout the entire Bay Area waterfront. Helicopters from CBS Wide World of Sports and KTVU television cruised overhead, their cameras all vying for a glimpse of the modern-day restaurateur's race boat, the *Benihana* in action.

Rocky Aoki, founder of the restaurant chain was bringing his race boat and a few racing competitors back to San Francisco Bay for a scrimmage before the big race in Florida later that summer. Three years prior, in almost the exact location, Rocky had raced a thirty-eight-foot Cougar catamaran and brushed death. During a test run at seventy miles per hour, the boat lost its trim and dived into a wave. Rocky suffered many life-threatening injuries. Everyone thought he was insane for racing here again.

Mr. Aoki arrived at the yacht club for appetizers and drinks, which I had the honor of catering. He was unapproachable, surrounded by club members and racing fans seeking autographs.

Finally, I decided it was time to meet this fellow culinary entrepreneur. After all, he seemed to be enjoying the teriyaki New York strip steak appetizers I had prepared. Pretty gutsy of me, since he knew a great teriyaki place that served a similar item.

I introduced myself as the chef and owner and asked him if he needed anything.

"Is this your teriyaki recipe?" Rocky asked, his mouth full.

"I perfected it a couple of months ago using a blender technique to incorporate all the seasonings into a tantalizing combination of flavor and tenderizer."

"How about you coming to work for me?"

I didn't need time to think about it. "Thanks, but I'm content being my own boss."

This is when the light flashed in my head. What a revelation. Here was the owner of Benihana's, Rocky Aoki, offering me a job in the only restaurant I ever wanted to work for, one that had denied me a position less than two years earlier.

My advice is this: don't waste another day. Use the champion within to draw closer to your destiny so you can begin to experience similar journeys. Looking back, I see he had something better planned for me. I just wasn't aware of it at the time.

In September of 1982, Rocky Aoki, driven by faith but without obedience, raced his thirty-five-foot Active Marine racer in the Kiekhaefer St. Augustine Classic in Florida. He suffered leg injuries when the boat hit a swell at eighty miles per hour and shattered into pieces. Shortly after his recovery, he announced his retirement from the sport of racing, referring to its potentially dangerous outcomes.

THE PLAYBOOK *for* SMALL BUSINESSES

The Ordained Path

What drives you? Do you know where your journey will lead? Do you want to know?

This chapter will help you find answers to these questions. All the authors of the New Testament had one thing in common: they focused, through their faith, on what they wanted to accomplish.

We must live by faith in order to receive the eternal life he has promised to those who have been faithful to him. Simply put, the answers to the three questions above lie in the strength of your faith. Do you believe God has ordained a path for you? Do you choose to follow it? Your destination is brought into focus before you embark on your journey if you have faith and are willing to obey his instructions.

People frequently ask what my next move will be. My answer is simple: wherever he wants me is where I'll be. If you are one to receive the anointing of his will, then you know exactly what I'm talking about.

Whenever I have deviated or disobeyed him, I have received his punishment. What is his punishment? It's something not working out in your life the way you thought it should.

Your parents probably disciplined you when you were a kid. I never thought lighting my backyard on fire while playing Squad Fifty-One would result in such severe disciplinary action. All I ever wanted was to be was a fireman when I grew up.

We all can relate. We've discovered things that work well

for us and things that don't. There's no doubt in my mind that I was placed here to help people. Not only do I enjoy this passion immensely, but he continually promotes me when I've completed a task he's destined for me.

Even the people within my close circle believe under their breath that I'm insane for giving away $2,000 every month. Referring back to chapter 2, "Salary Caps Shouldn't Matter," this is one way I can give my good fortune back to those who wish to pursue some of the same dream. My current "Champion Within" assignment is twofold. First, I need to wake up this sleepy country before it's too late and warn them that this is our only hope for financial freedom. Second, I need to assist those who wish to become independent through creatively managing their own successful businesses.

On the contrary, when I deviated or disobeyed him as illustrated in the last chapter, I was punished for not obeying his will. My newsletter, although successful, catered to the affluent market, so he painfully reminded me that was not where he wanted me. It became obvious to Mr. Aoki that racing speedboats in excess of seventy miles per hour was not where he belonged either. Providing service to his customers through his ninety successful restaurants was exactly where he ordained him to be. He did not design him to be a raceboat skipper.

Victory in your business will come only if he has ordained it for you and you choose to obey his instructions. Does this mean that only successful businesses are navigated by him? It's entirely possible.

Here's why: I can look around and see why the majority of businesses fail, thirty thousand of them a month in this country. The one common denominator in those failures is that the owners had little or no "champion within" mindset in their message. When asked why they failed, they responded, "I thought all I needed was some money and a great idea."

Without faith, you have no clear vision of your destiny. Without obedience, you have no rudder. You'll eventually fail. It's just a matter of time.

Here are seven ways to apply the "champion within" mindset and produce many successes while keeping failure to a minimum:

ASK FIRST

When implementing a new idea, I always ask, "Is this what you want me to do?" You recall my friends telling me, "Steve, publish a newsletter. The country needs it." I listened to them instead of my faith and disobeyed him. The result was a punishing reminder. Over one hundred calls to my headquarters that day reminded me that this was not where he had instructed me to be.

RESPECT YOUR ASSIGNMENT

My friend Sandy thought she would ride the tide and catch the latest craze. She started a daycare business, leaving her ordained day job as a golf pro only to discover she had disobeyed her faith regarding her assignment. Sandy quickly realized this was not where she belonged.

145

DECIDE WHO TO HELP

Our ministry attempts to help everyone. How do we decide who to help and who not to? Should I wait for him to direct me? For answers to these questions, seek your faith and remain obedient. Because I want to help everyone, I sometimes skip over this lesson, act prematurely, and create bigger problems for myself.

Michael came to us in need of a vehicle. After a quick interview, it became clear that he needed more time to gather stability in the workplace before we could finance him. He walked to the dealership, so transportation was obviously a serious issue.

Upon leaving, he asked about a Kia Sedona minivan that Juan had just driven onto the lot. I jokingly told Michael that I needed to find the two missing seats before I could sell this car. After all, who would purchase a minivan with no seats?

"I don't care that it doesn't have seats." Michael eyed the minivan with more desperation in his eyes than I could resist.

Without consulting anyone, I asked him, "You'd buy this without seats?"

He said he would. Back inside we went and closed the deal. After the sale, I told my staff I was going to enter a new page in the sales training manual entitled, "How to sell a vehicle with no seats." Everyone laughed except April.

Three days later, when April poked her head in my office, she had an I-told-you-so grin on her face. "Ken from the bank is holding on line three for you, Steve."

Ah, the punishment. Michael was on foot, and for good

reason. He had a suspended driver's license, which resulted in automatic termination of his loan.

How can we improve our hasty, irrational decisions? By listening to God. If you are aligned with him in faith, that first instinctual gut feeling will tell you that your decision is right.

SEE YOUR SETBACKS AS THE TRAINING YOU NEED IN ORDER TO EXPERIENCE VICTORY

Don't be discouraged if that promotion, job interview, or new business doesn't take hold when you believe it should. If you're walking in faith and willing to be patient, he probably has something far better waiting for you. For months, I dreamed of becoming a chef at Benihana's, but he had a different, better plan for me. Remember, faith is the assurance of things hoped for, the conviction of things not yet seen.

CUT YOUR LOSSES

When something isn't working, be willing to cut your losses. There is no telling how long he will allow punishment for your behavior. Learn to recognize mistakes quickly. Prideful tendencies keep us from admitting we made a wrong turn.

EXCEED EXPECTATIONS

Exceeding your customers' expectations is the only way your business will survive in these times. I boldly believe that the Christian principles taught throughout this book will align you with your faith and you'll recognize your champion within. Don't fall prey to doubt, for he who doubts is like a wave of the sea that is driven and tossed by the wind. Whatever the nature of your business, stimulate your mind and try different things, but always examine your faith in the project first, to determine which is the right thing to do at the right time.

Your customers will respond to a good idea! Six months before we opened our second location, we stopped every customer who came in to make a payment and asked what they thought about the idea. Interestingly, we received the positive feedback we'd hoped for. We made sure to thank everyone for their input. We let them know the second store is a hit and that their voices assisted in that process.

MAINTAIN YOUR CONNECTION

If you find yourself disconnected from the champion within, take the time to reestablish your connection. I'm happy to help. Many of my readers go to my blog to ask questions that I'm delighted to answer. Sometimes it's those little confirmations that lead us to reconnect. www.yourbusinessboost.com.

THE TAKEAWAY: Contrary to secular thinking, the opportunities for self-employment are far more abundant than they were just ten years ago. What's shattered that hope is the perception of business and how it is conducted. Universally, across all playing fields, the consumer has been sacrificed for greed and profit. The winning recipes are the lessons taught within the *Playbook*, and this is why the champion within will prevail.

Take the necessary steps to restore order and enjoy the opportunities you'll create through your efforts. Businesses may vary, but the consumers who patronize them stay the same. The number one reason a customer tells her tribe that your business is different from all the rest is how well you execute the image of "the champion within."

CHAPTER 12

RESTRAINT AND PATIENCE: DON'T FORCE THE THROW

THE DEFENSIVE LINE-UP: The gate is wide and the way is easy that leads to failure. Those who enter through it are many. Without hesitation, they ignore the warnings that lead away from disruption. How do I keep my business from this dismal statistic of failure?

OFFENSIVE STRATEGY: The gate is narrow and the way is hard that leads to success, and those who find it are few. The explanation is simple: the patience and restraint required to win don't come naturally. They may never evolve in the average person. They require great effort and must be practiced daily. You don't find success by striking oil in your backyard; rather, you become successful because you prevailed when turmoil struck in your front yard.

Like many fourteen-year-olds, I found that waiting for the lunch bell to ring was one of the highlights of my school day. Fortunately, I was dismissed from algebra class thirty minutes early because I was the lucky one chosen to serve lunch and wash dishes in the cafeteria.

Loping down the hall, I caught a whiff of cornmeal muffins. That meant at least twenty-five muffin pans sat soaking in a thirty-gallon sink because Mrs. Daisy never used non-stick spray.

I was their official whipping boy, these three older ladies dressed in white, wearing hair nets, patiently awaiting my pre-noon arrival. Scrubbing their pots and pans, mopping storeroom floors, washing down counters, scraping old gum off tables, and stocking deliveries in a blowing, twenty-degree deep freeze were just some of my duties. For this the school paid me seventy dollars per month. This was big, and it meant this teenager didn't have to con his mom or dad for spending money.

It was the first Tuesday in February, and my monthly paycheck had arrived to compensate my month's torture. After cafeteria duty, I had just enough time to scoot downtown before lunch ended and cash my check at the town's only bank, Bank of America. I had a crush on one of the tellers, Lori, who was always worth jeopardizing my punctual return to fifth period. As I entered, she called out my name, smiling in a way that always made me feel at least sixteen. I flirted shamelessly with Lori until someone approached the bank's only other teller window.

We've all been in this situation in a bank before. When

the teller calls the next customer to the window, we all look to see who walks up next to us. It's a normal reflex; after all, this is a bank, prone to getting robbed. Thinking this, I glanced to my right where the customer approached the window without being called, since no one was waiting in line.

This guy wore baggy camouflage pants, a huge coat, sunglasses, and a hat. *Is he going to rob the bank?*

As he slunk closer, he pulled his gloved hand from his left pocket and dropped a note on the counter. Then he raised his right hand, still in his jacket pocket, to the counter, motioning that he had a gun.

The teller read the scribble then let the note flutter to the counter, her mouth open. He motioned a second time as if to say he had a gun and would use it if she didn't give him all the money, now.

From the corner of my right eye, I saw this as an opportunity to take this guy down and become a hero. My adrenaline boiled. What should I do? I glanced over Lori's shoulder and saw that the only other employees sat at their desks, oblivious to what was going down.

The teller's hands trembled as she took all the money from her drawer and placed it on the counter. Time was ticking.

He put the money in his left pocket. She raised her hands in a gesture that said that was all there was. His frown told me he wasn't satisfied.

Was he going to do something life changing here? My pulse escalated as he backed away toward the entrance.

This was my chance. It was now or never. I took one step toward the door.

"I'm being robbed!"

The teller's voice stunned the thief. The split-second desperation in his eyes showed me he was thinking about stifling her. Thank God, he spun around instead and, like a running back in the NFL, jetted out the front door while shouting profanities at us.

At his quick departure, my heart rate slowed back to normal, and the rebound from the earlier adrenaline rush gave me that familiar sick, weak feeling. I realized that for once, I had a pretty good excuse for my tardiness in returning to school.

The next morning, an FBI agent called and informed me how lucky we were. This particular robber had a history of presenting his handgun and even had struck someone at a coffee shop.

The lead story on the front page of the next morning's *Mendocino Beacon* displayed the bank's photos of the robber and me side by side during the heist.

He was never caught.

Patience as a Virtue

It's a difficult pursuit, because our software, programmed from birth, sets us up for failure unless we learn the virtues of patience and restraint. The benefits of Spirit-fulfilled patience will provide successful decision making.

Augustine, the great bishop of the fourth century, said,

"We must indeed will to be patient, but patience as a genuine virtue comes only to those who have been redeemed by Christ and in whom the Holy Spirit is calling forth the fruit of the Spirit."

Patience and restraint, according to the Bible, are fruit of the Spirit. Eventually, if it's his will, the apple tree will bear fruit. If the Spirit of Christ is in us, we can expect the life of

> *"Most business failures are merely the result of impatient decision making."*

Christ to be lived out in us in the same way. The difference is that we must choose which gate, because we naturally default to our fleshly attitude. But how do we choose to be patient?

Take the bank robbery and its potential outcome, for example. This experience has stayed with me all my life. I use it to help me develop patience. In this example, intervention on my part would have had life-altering ramifications.

What if you started to envision your decision-making process as though your life depended on it? Have you had a life-altering experience? Imagine you were given a chance to relive it. Would you stop and weigh the potential outcomes with more diligence before you acted? I'll bet you would. In my case, opting not to pursue this armed robber was a prudent decision.

Most business failures are merely the result of impatient decision making. The more hasty decisions you make, the greater your failure. The more the failures, the quicker your business will cease to exist.

Before I begin my day, I think of a scenario, like my bank robbery experience. This establishes the attitude I'll have when my first decision arrives, usually before the doors to the dealership even open. In fact, my phones begin ringing about 7:30, since this is when the majority of my customers are leaving for work. My Wyoming store services over three hundred accounts. This means they make their payments and vent all problems here.

One morning, a customer named Heather, owner of a Hyundai Tiburon, called to inform me she has locked her keys in her car. The car happens to be running under her carport. "If you don't have an extra key and come over here now, how am I going to get to work on time?"

She purchased her car seven months ago and has been a satisfactory payer.

To keep from exploding on her, I remind myself of my near-death experience at Bank of America. Perhaps you don't have an armed robbery, but maybe you experienced a near-death car accident. Collect something with great imagery. This helps to instill restraint before you say or do something you'll later regret.

I challenge you to imprint one of your near-death experiences into your head. Perhaps you made a prudent decision. Maybe you didn't and its outcome allowed you to examine what went wrong. In other words, he has given you a second chance. This will act as your focus when you need patience and restraint to keep you from saying or doing the wrong thing—or from doing the right thing at the wrong time.

If you want to fail at business, treat your customers without priority. If you desire success, then patience and restraint are a must-win combination. People who criticize your business will at some point brew a recipe for your business' demise.

Heather happens to work for an Albuquerque call center that services thirty of our in-house financing referrals. It was imperative that I dash to her aid and unlock her car in hopes that she would inform her tribe of co-workers that the $5,000 Car Store genuinely cares about their customers. Later that month, we did receive another referral from her, which resulted in two additional car deals.

Word must have escaped. Darn! We make a duplicate key to every vehicle we sell. When a distressed customer calls, he's elated to discover he doesn't have to fork out sixty dollars for a locksmith. This generates at least two calls a week to the dealership (requiring patience and restraint), especially in the winter months when a single parent warms up her vehicle on a freezing morning before placing the young children in the backseat.

PATIENCE AND THE FUTURE

Throughout my adulthood, I've wondered how we as a nation are going to survive our old age and adequately provide for our children. Former U.S. Comptroller General David Walker said, "There will not be enough money available to service the aging needs of our seniors."

Only 4 percent of this population will be able to meet

the challenge without assistance. The choices are the government, your employer, or you, and that's it.

Which one will you place your hope in? No white knight will come to save you. This has always bothered me. My friends, the need for mobilization has never been greater. We have a responsibility not only to ourselves, but to our children as well. This current breakdown in our families can be corrected if we have the patience to start now. Our only hope is to restore the family structure with unity. We can do this by implementing the principles of this book.

How would you like to wake up every morning, knowing that your family's future is secure in your hands and not the government's, being navigated by you, not an employer? That's the question I pose to you today.

When I raise this question, most responses I receive are favorable, with one exception. "Yes, of course I would like to live that way. But how do I get started? I have no resources available."

The answer begins with patience and restraint, not hastily made monetary applications. Most people I counsel expect miracles overnight, and therein lies their demise. Here are some examples of patience and restraint that have led to great small-business successes and failures.

NINE YEARS IS NOT LONG; NEITHER IS ELEVEN

The average small business takes at least one year to go from paper to reality. Compared to a two-year AA degree, that's not bad. The $5,000 Car Store went from a full-time day job to a car dealership in ten months. Within nine years, we started a second store and have plans for eight additional stores. This took a total of eleven years.

Most People Quit Before Witnessing Success

One of my newsletter subscribers, Sarah from California, was very excited. She had just became a subscriber to my investment newsletter and received the December 1996 edition. It featured early recommendations to a company called Maverick Tube, symbol MAVK, traded on NASDAQ. The company manufactured metal tubular goods for the oil-drilling industry.

I had contacted the company's CEO, Mr. Gregg Eisenberg, on December 13. He detailed for me his strategy for the upcoming fiscal year. In his enthusiasm, he articulated his vision, which translated into something I could pass on to my subscribers for potentially huge stock gains. The recommendation was made. Everyone who purchased the stock that winter benefited as Mr. Eisenberg's prediction proved correct, resulting in stellar profits and a doubled stock price.

We should view investing in the stock market as a long-term strategy. Over time, history has demonstrated that companies producing profits on a consistent basis will deliver great returns to their shareholders. My investment strategy was similar to this, but targeted individual situations for a shorter term and bigger profit potential.

Sarah constantly called me. "When is this stock going to pop?"

Looking into my crystal ball, I told her Thursday the twentieth at exactly 3:00. Just kidding, but seriously, she called me about once a week to ask me that question.

Sad for her, her patience couldn't hold out. She sold her one thousand shares at one dollar over her purchase price. I believe her investment time in this company was a whole six weeks.

Fifteen days later, after an earnings release, the stock vaulted out of its base and continued a climb that would increase over 100 percent before the end of 1997.

Sarah's lack of restraint cost her over $13,000 that year.

THE HAROLD BENZ STORY

With beer always on his breath, Harold used to cruise by on his bicycle, asking Becky for a cigarette. After her departure, he'd happen by for some spare change and an occasional chat. Living in a teardrop trailer on his sister's property, with no running water or electricity, life had to be difficult for him. Harold was a pretty good paint-and-body guy when sober and willing to work. When he landed his old job back at Earl Scheib, a paint-and-body shop around the corner from the dealership, I saw him on a regular basis.

I knew that if we were ever going to expand our ability to purchase vehicles in volume, less expensive and with less competition, we would have to incorporate a paint-and-body presence. Convincing Harold to quit a job that tolerated his drinking, paid him great, allowed him to disappear, and provided both medical and dental benefits was difficult. What little patience he did possess was just enough to convince him things would work out.

I began buying, and Harold began painting our new, strategically purchased vehicles in the back of the dealership after hours. Aside from the toxic smell and dust everywhere, things worked out pretty well until one of my neighbors came over to inform me that some residue had drifted over to his property, covering his parked customer cars.

Thirty-five hundred dollars later, my neighbor's "vehicle restoration project" was completed. Moving our paint facility out of the dealership became top priority. I couldn't believe the negative attitudes we encountered. We offered everyone within a hundred feet of Harold's spray gun a free, albeit toxic, buzz every afternoon. We moved five different times in two years until acquiring the facility we occupy today. Harold, our foreman, and his girlfriend, crank out at least one vehicle per day. Because of his restraint, he hasn't had a drink in over two years and resides in the home I occupied until last year.

We're granted a limited amount of time here to fulfill the will he prescribed for our lives. Some people will receive it, and others won't. The saddest thing I can fathom is to believe that our faith is real but not complete the task because we don't have the patience.

THE TAKEAWAY: My used-car lot began in the driveway at my house. After three very successful months, Becky and our dog, Angel, convinced me that the increased traffic was giving our neighbors the impression that we were

Colombian-Cartel drug dealers. Becky ordered me to move my operation immediately.

The next stop was a busy street corner, which proved even better for business but very hazardous to my life. I knew if I could succeed at these locations, a retail storefront with street traffic and being legal would make me a sure-fire success.

My first commercial location was zoned C2, the legal jargon allowing for a car lot. It accommodated parking for one customer (barely) and six vehicle-display spaces. When the city's inspector came out to approve my permit, he drove right past me. I saw him slow down and look, much like my customers did. Then he circled the block and hesitantly pulled his vehicle into my only outside space.

I knew I was going to have the same battle with him as I did with my landlord, the dealers licensing bureau, bonding company, and banker. They all told me, "You'll never make it. You can't sell cars out of this tiny location."

The champion within told me different.

My friends, this start-up company is about two things: receiving the championship of faith (daring to be different) and being patient long enough to carry out the principles of the *Playbook* (exceeding my customers' expectations).

My assumption proved correct. The inspector didn't come within twenty feet of my building. Standing on the curb of the sidewalk, he smirked at me. "I can't approve this for a car lot. You'll never make it. I'm doing you a favor."

"I'll be the judge of that." I bit back the retort I wanted to make. I knew that legally, I was correct.

Several months later, after many trips downtown, I finally received the okay and opened my doors. Expanding beyond my expectations, we lived there for almost four years before moving to a facility five times larger.

In a similar situation, at first glance, all-pro quarterback Brett Favre seems to force the football into the hands of more defensive players than any other quarterback in history, earning him the dubious title of "all-time interception leader." But is this the result of risk taking and daring to be different or lack of patience and restraint? The fact of the matter is his percentage of pass attempts to interceptions is one of the all-time lowest, and he happens to be the NFL's leading passer.

A friend of mine wished to open his car dealership on this lot after my departure, but the city denied him a permit. To this day, the property sits vacant and dilapidated on historic Route 66.

Discipline yourself not to force the throw, but have the patience to win the game.

CHAPTER 13

LIVING IN THE RED ZONE

THE DEFENSIVE LINE-UP: Failure to cross the goal line when the opportunity arises is the result of not executing the proper play call while in your red zone. One of the reasons 70 plus percent of small businesses fail is because they don't practice this principle.

OFFENSIVE STRATEGY: When executing your business plan, do it with the intensity to win. You gain market share by providing superior service, calling the right plays, and producing a great product. This will lead to victory over your competition. You'll find this noteworthy because most businesses follow secular trends that lead only to profit-motivated agendas that ultimately deceive the customer. Many business owners never grasp this concept of playing to win in the red zone, but you will.

What is the red zone? It's the narrow window of opportunity all business owners experience just before the customer says "yes" or "no" to their product or service.

At the $5,000 Car Store, that pivotal moment is the test-drive. This narrow window of opportunity is when my customer decides whether to purchase or pass. We've discussed the requirements for our in-house financing and have determined that this customer can purchase here today. Once he's inside the vehicle, rolling down the road, there is no gray area. He will either love it or hate it. Our selection and execution of our play calls while inside our red zone determine whether we win the sale.

The first play calls in our arsenal today are number one, "The five-minute drill" and number seven, "Never rest on your laurels." In the five-minute drill, my staff and I strive to determine whether the customer can purchase today, and if not, whether we can solve one of her problems in five minutes or less.

In play call number seven, we keep in mind that although we may have the best price, service, and product, those alone won't guarantee victory. Therefore, in winter months, we always bring the vehicle up from its space and turn on the heater full blast so the car is nice and cozy-warm when the customer gets in. Likewise, in summer months, you'll notice a nice, cool cabin because the air conditioner will be blowing cold.

Obviously, it's imperative that the vehicle drive flawlessly, but it must also conform to the customer's lifestyle. At this point, we introduce play number six, "Discard the status quo." Prior to the test-drive, we conduct a short interview to determine the customer's creditworthiness. We also discover which radio station is his favorite. When he sits in his new car, he notices the song that's playing. It's one he likes, because the radio station is set to his favorite station. A fair number of potential buyers will pass if there's no stereo.

The next play call is number five, "Do not be afraid to risk the big play." Do not copy-cat other businesses in your industry. Shake things up. Before we hand over the vehicle, we slide back the front seats, adjust every mirror out of focus, turn the emergency flashers on, and roll down at least two windows. This play call forces the customer to readjust everything to her exact specifications, which results in a "taking-ownership" mindset before she rolls out of our driveway. A hint of fresh-linen fragrance wafts inside the vehicle, setting the tone for the perfect test-drive.

> *"Do not be afraid to risk the big play... Shake things up."*

The great sportswriter, Grantland Rice, once said, "It's not if you win or lose—it's how you play the game." This is a true statement, but if you prepare an effective strategy (execute and call the right plays) within your red zone, you'll score enough to win.

My customers are similar to yours. Most have taken the time to become knowledgeable about the product or service you offer. The Internet has become instrumental in educating them, not only about the vehicles they're interested in, but also how we as a company deliver and service them.

The play call we use next is number four, "Always have a vision of the goal line." We place the jubilant customer into a perfectly performing vehicle. Then we make sure that when she returns it to the dealership after the test-drive, she is greeted with great service and humble attitudes. We score within our red zone 92 percent of the time. This means the customer departs in her vehicle, ecstatic—off to share the experience with friends, family, and co-workers.

If we're lucky enough, the customer has visited one of our competitors first and has test-driven one of their vehicles, discovering a "service engine soon" light illuminated. All the better if the car had a rough idle, an unidentifiable stench coming from the backseat, and a severe pull to the left when he let go of the steering wheel.

We are confident that our customers will not find any imperfections in the vehicles they drive at our stores. We spend eighty yards (the equivalent of at least three days) marching down the field to get there (preparing that vehicle for sale), but the last twenty yards or the "red zone" (about half an hour) determine whether we're fortunate enough to win their business.

It's possible you've never watched a football game in your life. Once a woman approached me and asked what a goal line was. She did know her stats; she informed me that 52 percent of all new business owners in this country last year were female. My wife, Becky, understands victory but couldn't care less about the gridiron. No one takes more seriously the proliferation of women into small business than I do.

My passion is placing my fresh-baked cookies onto a shelf low enough for all to receive them. I'm not here to try to mold you, rather unfold you. Managing a small business isn't a game. My dear friends, I don't want anyone to fail, but I believe these waters hold much failure. The odds are that most won't survive, but you will. This is why on my blog I always encourage questions, which I'm happy to answer.

Jennifer and her significant other, Rosa, own a flower shop where I purchase all my special-occasion bouquets. Their execution is simple yet effective. They cater to small business owners and entrepreneurs, aware that our time is stretched. The big play they used in their red zone to capture my business was brilliant. It was number five, "Don't be afraid to risk the big play." Somehow, they discovered when my anniversary was and sent me a letter of congratulations. At first glance, it appeared as though it was from Becky because it included a cute reminder of what could happen if I forgot. Finding it amusing, I blew it off.

The next contact came a few days later. Again, it looked like something my wife would send me. Persistent they were, convinced I wasn't—until the next correspondence arrived. It was a mock-up of a letter from an attorney, specializing in divorce cases. Bold and creative, it worked. I called their shop.

Jennifer and Rosa will meet with you at your place of

work and complete a special-event journal for every occasion of significance. On the average, most people have seven special occasions and one surprise that unfold within a year. This shop sends out e-mail notifications two weeks before the special day and takes care of all the details. Being a client of theirs, I'm ensured that I will always look good by never forgetting.

The play calls they use and execute brilliantly are number four ("Always have a vision of the goal line") and number five ("Don't be afraid to risk the big play"). Jennifer and Rosa have literally abolished my fear of forgetfulness by providing reliable, creative, and bold service with a superior product. Their business grows about 20 percent per year.

FAILURE IN THE RED ZONE

The house was a palace, the grounds impeccable. You'd expect to see architecture like this in Allahabad, India, not nestled among the trees and landscape of modern-day Albuquerque. The occasion: to celebrate India's Independence Day.

Inside, sixty guests, comprising mostly the East Indian "who's who" of Albuquerque commerce, waited for the mayor to arrive. Mannequins in full military dress, gold religious statues, swords, and other native Indian artifacts adorned the lower floor. Ancient history books and thousands of medical books filled the four-hundred-square-foot library.

Dr. Abdula Kasheem, the owner of this beautiful home,

and his family have lived here for ten years. Dr. Kasheem is responsible for the day-to-day operations of two major hospitals in the state of New Mexico.

His accolades include initiating the Helo-Life Flight program, which consists of two patient-transport helicopters capable of landing in an area no bigger than the average rooftop. The helicopters withstand winds up to forty miles per hour and are credited with saving up to 750 lives since the program's inception seven years ago. With New Mexico's open landscape consisting of 121,598 square miles, every minute counts. Dr. Kasheem also directs one of the largest pediatrics wards in the United States, is responsible for recruiting several highly skilled surgeons from his native homeland, and has overseen additions to both hospitals totaling 600 new rooms.

At last, Mayor Martin "Marty" Chavez, dressed in casual clothing, strode through the double-plated glass doors of Dr. Kasheem's home. Recently named one of the top "World Mayors of North America," he worked the crowd, shaking hands and thanking everyone for coming. Several weeks before, he had announced that he would run for his fourth term as mayor of Albuquerque.

The menu that night consisted of spicy East Indian food. Not wanting to be rude in the company of the mayor, I ate everything on my plate and paid the price throughout the entire next week.

After our meal, Mayor Marty stood. "The recent presidential election has taken the enthusiasm away from the regional races. The upcoming gubernatorial and mayoral elections across the country are predicted to encounter the lowest turnouts in over twenty-five years, resulting in very tight races."

This didn't sound like the usual victory-confident Mayor Marty I had only watched on television before tonight. Downplay is a brilliant strategy for any politician, but sometimes it can backfire.

I shook his hand and whispered into his ear, "If you need a great example of what you've done in Albuquerque for small business, call me and let's shoot a commercial. I promise that this testimonial will have a lasting impact on the business community."

I gave him my card and truly expected to hear from him. With the recent economic downturn, I figured he could use me as an example. He chose not to execute within his red zone. Too bad, Mr. Mayor, for victory was granted to a more formidable competitor.

RED-ZONE PLAY CALLS THAT BRING SUCCESS

Here are seven play calls I execute within my red zone. Perhaps they can work for you too. The recipe for producing a wildly successful business is about to get really interesting.

THE FIVE-MINUTE DRILL

When a customer asks what's unique about your business and why he should purchase your product or service, you must give the answer in five minutes or less. Tell him in a way that he can convey this message to his friends, family, and co-workers.

Verizon Wireless, where I receive my cellular service, makes it clear what they do, but Lupe, the store manager and a 5K customer, executes this strategy brilliantly. She leaves no room for doubt. In a five-minute drill, she explains all the plans and services. I can go home and tell Becky what I did and why.

If you can't convey your passion, purpose, and mission concisely, how do you expect your customers to do so? Rehearse this technique with your entire staff. Everyone should share the same answer and enthusiasm. There's nothing worse than being told two completely different stories by two different staff members.

WHILE IN YOUR RED ZONE, DO YOU HAVE YOUR GAME FACE ON?

When Mayor Marty stood, it was clear that he didn't have his game face on, nor was he operating in his red zone. He appeared lethargic to his audience.

Want to see what a real game face looks like? Type http://tinyurl.com/yc30h53. It depicts the intensity of a true game face, (your daily walk in your business). On Jan 19, 2002, in a snow-covered Foxboro, Massachusetts stadium, Mr. Brady was chased by Oakland Raider defensive player Rod Coleman. Brady led his team to a stunning, come-from-behind overtime victory in that AFC championship game. If this site still exists, it's worth a peek. Photo taken by: Ezera Shaw/Getty.

CALL THE RIGHT PLAY

Yes, it's a theatre play, scripted especially for your team. The casting of your staff is crucial, as is the script they will follow. What sets apart championship teams from the mediocre is how well they are coached and how they execute their red-zone plays. Practice and rehearse your message. The only excuse for failure is not being prepared for success.

ALWAYS HAVE A VISION OF THE GOAL LINE

After Alan Alda reassured me that I was where I belonged, I never looked backward. There's a good reason the rear-view mirror in your car is one-fiftieth the size of your windshield. Don't focus on the past. Keep your target in the cross hairs in front of you. The decisions you make will result in victory.

DON'T BE AFRAID TO RISK THE BIG PLAY

How will you know whether you've called the big play at the correct time? Simple: imagine what your customer might be thinking. Place yourself on the other side of the desk, counter, phone, or aircraft.

A few years ago, I had the opportunity to fly with an airline in which a friend of mine was first officer. Could you imagine the look on my face as I boarded the aircraft, peeked into the flight deck, and saw Hank winking at me?

Since we'd waited over an hour to board, my cabin-mates were already edgy, and Hank and I didn't want to stall the line out. So we shook hands, exchanging pleasantries, as I shuffled along to my seat.

I knew Hank pretty well. A joker was he by nature, but I didn't think he would attempt anything goofy while on duty. *Or would he?*

You know the feeling we fleshly beings like, the one of relevance? We all like to be recognized as someone special, don't we? I'm no different.

As soon as we reached flying altitude, there went Hank. "Good afternoon, ladies and gentlemen. Greetings from the flight deck. We have a very special guest on board with us."

Ugh. Surely he won't—I slumped down in my seat.

"It's Steve Henry. You might know him as one of the best investment advisors in the country. He recommended the purchase of this airline in his most recent news-letter."

When we landed, I received an airline standing ovation and requests for my business cards.

Risking the big play involves creativity and the willing-ness to stir things up. You'll never experience a champion-ship victory without it. When I received divorce papers from an attorney, it got my attention. I called my florist right away.

DISCARD THE STATUS QUO

When returning home one afternoon, I walked across the street to catch a cab. Directly in the middle of the line

STEVE HENRY

was a cabbie dressed like a pirate. He had a cockatoo perched on his shoulder, an eye patch covering his right eye and the wardrobe to match. Interesting.

As I approached the lineup, the bird screeched at me. "Over here, sir. Yes, you. I'm talking to you!"

This bird got my attention, enough to lure me to the pirate cabdriver. The rest was history. I fetched a ride home and was entertained the whole way there. Gil and Mad Dog (named after his great dog-barking impersonations) claim they have more fun with new mail carriers. (Hmm) They deliver more passengers to more destinations than any other cabbie in the state.

When asked how, Gil says, "We're a little different."

NEVER REST ON YOUR LAURELS

We may be the best at serving our customers, but that doesn't keep me from thinking about a family-owned movie-rental store in my neighborhood. Bob, Jan, and daughter Sue operated successfully and treated their customers with team spirit at Valley Video for eight years.

Then the big blue box store (Blockbuster Video) arrived on the scene. The 10,000-square-foot building, made of stand-alone brick and mortar, resided in the same strip center and brought disaster to the mom-and-pop operation. Less than two years later, 80 percent of Valley Video's customer base eroded away. Bob and Jan were forced to close their store. Funny thing: eight years later, that Blockbuster sits as an empty shell, teetering on the edge of bankruptcy.

Their demise originates from new competition from video-on-demand and this red kiosk that spits out movies to customers who wait in line up to five minutes inside a grocery store. No business can withstand the winds of change and live to tell about it unless they refuse to rest on their laurels.

Never forget to ask your customers, "What can we do to keep your business?"

THE TAKEAWAY: The parable of the Good Samaritan, revised to portray a small-business attitude:

A lawyer had tried to test Jesus, asking what he might do to inherit eternal life. Jesus answered, "You must love your God with all your heart, soul, mind and strength and love your neighbor as yourself."

"Just who is a neighbor?" the curious lawyer asked.

"Here's an example," came the reply. "A certain man was going down from Jerusalem to Jericho and fell among robbers, who both stripped him and beat him and then departed, leaving him half dead. By chance, a certain priest was going down that way. When he saw him, he passed by on the other side. In the same way a Levite also, when he came to the place, saw him and passed by on the other side. But a certain Samaritan, as he traveled, came where he was. When he saw him, he was moved with compassion, came to him, and bound up his wounds, pouring oil and wine. He set him on his own animal, brought him to an inn, and took care of him. On the next day, when he departed, he took out two denarii, gave them to the host, and said to him, 'Take care of him. Whatever you spend beyond that, I will repay you when

I return.' Now which of these do you think seemed to be a neighbor to him who fell among the robbers?"

The lawyer answered, "He who showed mercy on him."

Then Jesus said to him, "Go and do likewise."

Here is the cast as it should play out in small-business management:

The Victim: Your customer

The Levite and the Priest: The way your competitors view things

Eternal Life: Your successful, humbly managed business

Your neighbor: I hope it's you

Executing the play calls within your red zone won't result in anything unless you're doing them for all the right reasons. The next chapter reveals this meaning: "Go and do likewise."

CHAPTER 14

THE SECRET PLAYS REVEALED

THE DEFENSIVE LINE-UP: How can you raise the bar for the entire team the way high tide raises all boats in a harbor?

OFEENSIVE STRATEGY: You've scattered seeds into good soil and seen miracles of victory among the people who make up your team. Sadly, only one in four reaps the harvest; hence, the 70-plus percent business failure rate. You can learn to provide an environment in which management, employees, and suppliers help produce the ultimate harvest of one hundredfold. To those who understand this parable, it won't be a secret anymore.

When we ponder how to produce this bumper crop, it's important to note what the outcome will look like. Once the harvest is in and your employees and customers see your vision to victory, they will become addicted to your company's future and forget the status quo they knew before. If they backslide, they won't stay away long. The culture you'll create is the good soil that will benefit all who understand these secrets. The addiction you form will become an influence that lasts a lifetime. As the business owner, you'll spend ample time preparing five plays in hopes that all will receive.

An outsider, Chuck (our stereo and GPS installer) explained this concept to Tony, my recon manager. As Tony tossed a Krispy Kreme doughnut into the microwave, Chuck gave him a sly grin. "What would you do if Steve didn't have those doughnuts today? He's got you all addicted!"

Chuck's exactly right. At 5:00 a.m. every Wednesday, I drive twenty miles out of my way to Krispy Kreme and buy unstuffed doughnuts before they're filled with custard. They're fluffed up and laced twice with the sugary glaze, in preparation for stuffing but without any filler (and available only in the pre-dawn mornings). If you haven't made previous arrangements with night management, you probably won't ever see them. I plan to sell several cars to the employees at Krispy Kreme for turning me on to these sugar-glazed pillows.

What product or service do you provide to express your thanks, care, and love to your team? Tony's answer to Chuck was "I'm not sure. If Steve passed away, I'd have to ask April."

Your staff's expectation of the bar moving higher has to be greater than their current experience. After eight consecutive Wednesdays, I became aware that the bar was not moving higher. So I introduced another fantastic morning offering: Einstein bagels with my homemade roasted red and green chili cream cheese.

Leaders who prepare the good soil know that tomorrow's meal has to be better than yesterday's. The next vehicle a customer purchases from the $5,000 Car Store has to be better than the last. When Rosa delivered my wife's birthday roses, Becky called me and said, "They're the most beautiful I've ever seen."

> *"What product or service do you provide to express your thanks, care, and love to your team?"*

When I take my first bite of a Gaucho's large green chili and sausage pizza, it has to be better than I remember from last time. When my friend Chip MacGregor (*Publisher's Weekly's* number one literary agent of 2009) negotiates a book deal, the publishers expect something greater than he submitted before. He told me, "If I submit a manuscript with less-than-perfect writing, they may excuse me once and wonder, *hmm—is he losing it?* But never will they forgive me twice." The pursuit of pleasing and winning keeps the bar constantly rising and ensures an abundant harvest.

The clear objective is to advance your entire team, using the bar as your barometer. I've spoken to many business owners who truly believe I'm the one who doesn't hear these words: "People work for us, not themselves. This economy doesn't allow me to invest in them by purchasing special gifts or treating them like royalty, and lunch? You've got to be kidding, I'm barely holding on."

I have a few questions for them. "Is your company setting any records? Do you have to resort to advertising in order to get your phone to ring? How many of the W-2s that you sent out last year came back with the address unknown? Are you expanding in this economy? Are you saddled with debt?"

Good soil must have the right ingredients working in tandem. Here are the five secrets that bring forth perfect soil. Using only a couple, you may muddle through, but all five are necessary to ensure that the bumper crop takes hold. Many forces will try to keep you from producing that one hundred-fold harvest.

HUMILITY

C.S. Lewis' definition of humility is the best I've heard. It's short but to the point: "Humility is not thinking less of yourself; it's thinking of yourself less." It's also not a bad idea to admit when we're wrong.

For example, Gail Young was running fifteen minutes late for her Los Angeles flight when her taxi pulled up curbside and dropped her off. Dashing through the airport, she realized she hadn't eaten a thing all day. She snatched a novel and a small bag of cookies from the CNN Newsstand and tossed a twenty onto the counter, then she raced to the TSA checkpoint. As she boarded the almost-filled-to-capacity aircraft, she spotted an empty seat next to a gentleman who occupied the window seat.

The plane commenced rotation and lifted off. Gail pulled out her book and opened her bag of cookies. Watching her out of the corner of his eye, the gentlemen also reached over, grabbed a cookie from the open bag, and ate it.

Appalled, Gail glared at him. How dare he eat her cookies! She grabbed a second cookie and watched as he did the same. The audacity of this man—taking her cookies without even asking.

She peered into the sack. Only one cookie remained. The man reached into the bag and pulled out the last cookie, broke it evenly down the middle, and placed her half onto her tray.

Have you ever been so angry you couldn't speak? That was exactly how she felt until she opened her purse to put her book away. Tucked inside was *her* bag of cookies, exactly where she had placed it as she hurried through the safety checkpoint.

We're so quick to assume we are right and the other person is wrong. "It's not my fault; it's his." We must learn to recognize our weaknesses, admit to them, and find a way to remedy them. People are always telling me I'm too soft and easygoing, that I let people roll right over the top of me. In fact, when one of our customers requests a payment arrangement with me, he must travel past the trip wire at April's desk to get to mine. She's an expert at sniffing out possible trouble and will activate the wire before they come within ten feet of me. Some people wait until she leaves for the day or will get by with a disabled vehicle until Saturday, knowing that is April's day off. I'm not allowed to release any codes or make payment arrangements without April's approval. I will, however, help anyone with a vehicle repair or problem.

I have a saying: "I make more mistakes in one day than most people make in a lifetime." I'm wrong most of the time. I admit I rely on my staff to answer the technical questions about the things I don't know. I'm perfectly content with this, for I operate a successful business in an industry that is disdained by many, but I'm setting records every month. My friends, this is living proof that it's not me, it's what flows through me as I use my giftings and these five secrets.

Stop focusing on what the other person may be doing wrong and fix your own mistakes. You'll achieve a lot more success when you focus your energy on the real problem: yourself.

If You Don't, No One Else Will

Spoil your employees and customers rotten by providing them with good soil. This economy is the perfect time to display your kindness, love, and compassion toward your team. I love the reputation of the used-car business. Some of it may be warranted, but look at the opportunity it provides to display our side. Do you see where your industry's reputation can provide you with these opportunities? Yelling, "Fire!" in an empty movie theater won't have much of an impact, but shoot a gun in the air at a crowded one and watch what happens next.

Mike, who bought a car from me a year ago, brought me another customer from Rio Twenty-One, the largest movie theater in New Mexico. (Mike takes full advantage of our in-house customer-referral program.) When I looked over his co-worker's application, I noticed both had worked there almost three years. What's unusual is that they make only nine bucks an hour. These kids are sharp, energetic, and in no way associated with criminal activities. I couldn't help but ask, "What keeps you there and why?"

"The wait to get a job there is up to six months," Mike said.

This was one of the first indicators that these men were part of a championship team. The reason they succeed is simple: they receive "royal treatment." For example, they get to watch all the new movies for free in the VIP room. This is a room with leather recliners, a sound system and screen that compare to IMAX, an open self-serve popcorn display, and a fountain of thirty different beverages. On Monday nights, the management allows the staff to bring one guest, and they too receive the treatment. Mike indicated that his dating schedule remains booked a month in advance.

The 5K is a firm executer of this principle. Our rewards include housing, transportation, and a great meal, to name a few. Another benefit that arises naturally from this act of team appreciation is the victory that some of my staff experience for the first time in their lives. I hope every one of you will experience the exhilaration of raising the human bar and witnessing the results.

Brand Yourself

It's been years since someone drove onto our dealership and asked to see a new vehicle or something we've never carried. Why is this? It's because our purpose is firmly branded within our culture, allowing everyone to know what we represent. When I check out my competition, I often see economy cars, large pickup trucks, and motor homes all on the same lot. I have to ask, what is it they do?

We need to maintain consistency. Restaurants, for example, don't offer barbeque one week and Chinese the next. It's okay to distinguish yourself from the rest of the herd, but do not deviate from your message.

We refer to ours as the "5K way." What is 5K? It's offering lunch to everyone who enters our stores. It's helping others accomplish their goals. It's growing daily in our faith. It's providing a healthy, positive environment in which to expand our model. It's never forgetting who pays the bills. It's constantly seeking ways to exceed our customers' expectations. It's never allowing the bar to get rusty from lack of upward movement. It's putting others first, even when they've locked themselves out of their car and it's not our fault. It's empowering our staff to become the best they can be. It's providing affordable, economical transportation to people who otherwise couldn't drive.

PERSONAL RELATIONSHIPS

The key ingredient in great relationships is the realization that no one person is above another. The presiding judge of the Fort Bragg courthouse found this out one day when he looked out his office window and saw five young boys arguing on the sidewalk. The judge stalked outside to break up this disagreement. "What's all the commotion about?"

The boys' leader stepped forward. "We're trying to decide who gets to take this stray dog home. The one who can tell the biggest lie wins!"

"I can't believe this," the judge said. "When I was your age, I never told lies. In fact, I spent all my time seeking only the truth."

The boys huddled for a moment, then their leader emerged again. "We all agree; you win. You get to take the dog home."

It's easy to judge and accuse others of crimes we can't imagine ourselves committing. Perhaps we should spend more time pondering the fact that we're all created in the same image. What if we sought opportunities to promote people instead of looking for ways to argue or tear one another down? Sometimes you'll be surprised to find the least obvious person needing your assistance.

L.J., drummer in a famous American rock band, once stated, "I put on my pants just like the rest of you: one leg at a time. But the difference is that once they're on, I make gold records. It's hard to believe—I perform in front of thousands of fans every week, receive letters and cards from thousand of people I've never met, but when I'm by myself, I'm the loneliest person in the world. I wish I had just one true friend."

I know L.J. (not his real name). He's the band's leader. His team wants to raise the bar but doesn't know how. You see, L.J. doesn't believe in personal relationships, for he's never known one. This makes it difficult to convey the relationship message to him. L.J., I hope this book helps you find what you're looking for. I believe that special relationship you're seeking can be found only in Jesus Christ.

Your team needs you to instill into them a spirit of patience, kindness, and fellowship. They rely on you to be their friend (sometimes impossible), so make the decision today to be that extraordinary person they look up to and seek leadership from. I've never seen a team win the championship game with a coach who didn't understand the true meaning of relationships. We're all in this battle together; we need each other. No team ever enjoyed victory from the efforts of a single player.

GIVE SOMETHING BACK

There won't be a U-Haul following the hearse in your funeral procession. Your earthly processions will remain here. When I look back on my career, I'm struck to believe that I truly had anything to do with my success. Don't get me wrong; it's me in the physical body, performing the duties that led me to arrive here. However, I'm driven by what flows through me, not by what I've done.

I worked a sales job for a large car dealership before I

started the 5K. Every couple of months, corporate employees flew in and allowed us to caddy their golf games by day and show them the town by night. The only joy those "good ole days" bring is when I consider how lucky I was to escape when I did. These fellows had no clue. They dictated policy from their corporate mahogany desks on the fifth floor of the home building. Oblivious to the realities of daily life in the trenches, these men and their condescending attitudes gave me the idea of starting my own dealership, using the opposite philosophy. On the other hand, their soil consisted of the status quo.

Every month, through the publishing arm of another company I own, I give away $2,000 to a business that registers on my website, www.YourBusinessBoost.com. An outside firm randomly selects a winner. It's my way of giving something back in hopes of helping other small businesses receive some capital on which to grow.

Discover ways to cultivate your harvest back into the good soil. Nurtured correctly, your prosperity will be plentiful. Become neighborly and give some of your harvest to others. There may not be a U-Haul, but the good soil you leave for the next farmer will have your seeds within.

THE TAKEAWAY: Here's a lesson that Jesus taught to his disciples and the multitudes that came to hear him, paraphrased from Mark 4:1-20. It should directly impact the way you choose to operate your business.

And a great crowd gathered around him and literally cornered him on the beach, so he got into a boat and began to teach beside the sea. And he was teaching them many things in parables, and in his teaching he said to them: "Listen! A farmer went out to sow. And as he sowed, some seed fell along the path, and the birds came and devoured it. Other seed fell on rocky ground, where it did not have much soil; immediately it sprang up, since it had no depth of soil. And when the sun rose, the seed was scorched, and since it had no root, it withered away. Other seed fell among thorns, and the thorns grew up and choked it, and it yielded no grain. And other seeds fell into good soil and produced grain, growing up and increasing and yielding thirtyfold, sixtyfold, and a hundredfold." And he said, "He who has ears to hear, let him hear." And when he was alone, those around him with the twelve asked him about the parable. And he said to them, "To you has been given the secret of the Kingdom of God, but for those outside, everything is in parables, so that they may indeed see but not perceive, and may indeed hear but not understand, lest they should turn and be forgiven."

And he said to them, "Do you not understand this parable? How then will you understand all the parables? The farmer sows the word. And these are the ones along the path, where the word is sown: when they hear, Satan immediately comes and takes away the word that is sown in them. And these are the ones sown on rocky ground: the ones who, when they hear the word, immediately receive it with joy. And they have no root in themselves, but endure for a while; then, when tribulation or persecution arises on account of the word, immediately they fall away.

And others are the ones sown among thorns. They are

those who hear the word, but the cares of the world and the deceitfulness of riches and the desires for material things enter in and choke the word, and it proves unfruitful. But those that were sown on the good soil are the ones who hear the word and accept it and bear fruit, thirtyfold, sixtyfold, and one hundredfold."

Here's how this parable relates to the managing of your small business. The farmer is you, the business owner; the seeds are the word, which is accepting and implementing the five secrets.

The seed along the path, trodden underfoot, is quickly eaten by the birds. These are the ones who allow others to dictate their destiny for them. My neighbor, John Ramsey, allowed his friends and relatives to push him into opening a business that failed because it wasn't his gifted will. John took their advice instead of keeping the passion a hobby. Remember; this happened to me too.

The ones along the rocky pathway get it—sort of—and think owning a business is a great way to make lots of money. They enjoy their newfound freedom but lack the conviction of following the plan that produces the secret plays. When trials and tribulation arise, it's not fun anymore. They'd rather do it their way. They believe in the here and now, the trends of the times, Monday through Friday, 9:00 to 5:00. Remember Sandy, the golf-instructor-turned-day-care-provider?

The ones who attempt to grow among the thorny bushes soon get choked out. They believe and implement the five secret plays—for a while. Then when things begin to thrive, greed enters in and mistakes proliferate. These people believe that a new car, 3000-square-foot house, and sailboat are necessary assets to show off their wildly successful business to their friends. The only problem is that they lost sight of the secret plays and got caught up in the riches and distractions of the world.

The ones who arrive in good soil and take root are the ones who have read this book and desire to coach a championship team, never lowering the bar. You've taken the proper time to hone your craft and sharpen your skills. You are the producers. You'll watch the harvest increase one hundredfold.

My dear friends, these principles are for those who seek a better life for their family. Remember; only one in four succeed, according to the parable. You are chosen. Very few receive the call to pass through the narrow gate. As God is my witness, I urge you to introduce these teachings into your business today. You'll see tremendous, profound results immediately. I wish the very best for you and have a passionate desire for victory for you and your business.

CHAPTER 15

THE HOME FIELD ADVANTAGE

DEFENSIVE LINE-UP: Making your fans your top priority when playing at home helps to guarantee a win when playing on the road. If your fans at home aren't relevant or satisfied, you'll enjoy fewer victories. Are you committed to your fans?

OFFENSIVE STRATEGY TAKEN: Enthusiastic fans give you more tallies in the "win" column. You'll be on top of your game if your fans know they share first place with you. Accomplish this by making every day Fan Appreciation Day. Enjoy the benefits of a home-field advantage when your fans root for you, when you tackle difficult problems, or when you play on the road.

What is a victorious road game? It's the confidence to compete and win in challenging times while surrounded by opposition.

Last September, I was returning home from a writers' conference in Spokane, through Seattle, to Albuquerque. While I was standing in line for a gate pass at Spokane's airport, I couldn't help noticing dozens of blue-painted faces. Hmm this was interesting.

Then a disgruntled Seahawk held by another man with a blue face, screeched in her cage and gave me my first clue. The Seattle Seahawks must be playing at home today.

As I boarded the plane, I realized that if anyone asked, I'd better acknowledge that I knew who the Seahawks were. Fatigued yet excited from my own weekend, all I wanted to do was find a seat, avoid these crazed fans, and digest my notes from the conference.

However, as I peered down the aisle, I knew that was never going to happen. It looked as if I had somehow walked onto the team's private plane. I had never seen anything like this. At least seventy fans partied in the plane, dressed in Seahawk blue and blowing a horn that was supposed to emulate a Seahawk and was ideally meant for an outside stadium, not for the inside of a 737 aircraft.

I had no choice but to find a seat and assume the team spirit. What ensued over the next hour was the loudest, most obnoxious Seahawk-screeching flight I've ever experienced. I couldn't believe the airline put up with the noise and disruption. According to one of the flight attendants, this takes place on ten flights across the Northwest every morning there's a Seahawk home game.

Unable to avoid this pregame pep rally, I leaned across the armrest to shout at my face-painted seatmate. "The stadium must be crazy too, huh?"

He informed me that Quest Field, where the Seahawks play, is known as the Stadium from Which the Twelfth Player Plays. Built in 2002 by Paul Allen, Quest Field got its nickname because it's the noisiest stadium in the country. (It's said that this was unintentional, but many wonder.) The noise from the home-field fans makes the visiting team think there must be twelve men on the field, not the legal eleven. As a result, visiting teams incur the most false-start penalties in the league. The visiting team also has problems executing effectively because of the noise. Management went so far as to retire their team's jersey number twelve. The name on the back reads, "The Fans."

"It's not only the noise," Seahawks defensive end Patrick Kerney said. "It's the enthusiasm these fans exude. It's kind of a perfect storm."

When the new Seahawks stadium opened in 2002, head coach Mike Holmgren wanted to give Seattle a true home-field advantage, so he implemented the fan-frenzied formula that successful teams use in the annual battle for NFL supremacy.

Eight years later, Quest Field has lived up to its moniker as the loudest stadium in the country, giving the home-field advantage to the Seahawks. Since 2003, only one team in the league—the perennial powerhouse New England Patriots—can boast of a better home record than Seattle. League-wide, home teams have won 57 percent of their home games, while the Seahawks' magic number is 81 percent.

The Seattle franchise knows it has an important tool in its arsenal. Their management team gets it: the fans comprise the home-field advantage that unequivocally produces more victories for the Seahawks. They have sold out over sixty consecutive games dating back to 2003. Does your company turn away business like this? Fourteen thousand tickets go on sale before every game, and they sell out in less than fifteen minutes. The remaining seats go to season-ticket holders.

You can bet that Paul Allen provides several benefits to his customers in order to keep that stadium full. Does he subsidize plane fares for his fans to reach the stadium on game day? It's possible. Do you think he has a list of at least six plays he uses to keep his fans believing they are his first priority?

Head coach Tom Flores coached these Seahawks (1992-1994) in their former home, the Kingdome. In a recent correspondence, Tom informed me, "Seattle has the most noise-conscious fans, in all of pro sports. Roaring crowds are not new, however. Knowledgeable uproars have become an art. An art the Seahawk fans have and are proud of. I was on both sides of this phenomenon, as a coach and a fan. Believe me when I tell you, it has an effect. It's a definite advantage."

THE 5K HOME-FIELD ADVANTAGE

What are you doing to attract your fans and keep them number one on your priority list? We sign fifty contracts per month with return customers (our season-ticket holders) at the $5,000 Car Store. This makes up 60 percent of our monthly sales, and it's a result of keeping these fans relevant and fulfilled. It's a great feeling to know that fifty customers will purchase vehicles at the $5,000 Car Store next month because of our home-field advantage. Our "away games" are the new business we must continue to capture every month. We must win these games too, which would be impossible without the home-field advantage.

Here are six daily practice points I use to show my fans it's their day—every day. In return, they show their support to my team by telling their friends, family, and co-workers where to purchase their next vehicle.

REMEMBER THEM BY THEIR FIRST NAME
AFTER THREE YEARS

For those of you who, like me, can't seem to remember what transpired yesterday, how is this possible? This is what the $5000 Car Store does: after we make a sale, we take a snapshot of the customer next to her new vehicle, and we pin the picture to the wall. The first thing everyone sees when they open our lobby door is a collage of 100 devoted fans smiling after their recent purchase.

My team also quizzes each other on who's who. They remind each other of details they noticed while selling a car.

If your business doesn't cater to retail traffic, consider my friend Stephanie, the successful housecleaner. She takes the time to ask for her clients' birth dates, as well as those of their children. When the client returns to her sparkling house, she finds a birthday card and small gift for the birthday person. Stephanie takes the time to make them feel special. She keeps a book of this vital information to let her fans know they're in first place.

How would you feel if you walked into a business after shopping elsewhere for the past three years and the staff still called you by name? Has this ever happened to you? Very few business owners receive this lesson. Jesus said, "Those who find it are few."

You'll see this confirmed time and time again, but not on the 5K's website—because I don't have one. However, my fans post their comments in the review section of the Internet. One of my repeat customers, "Cricket," confirmed this in the review she gave us on February 5.

ACKNOWLEDGE THEIR SUPPORT IN SUPER STYLE

Once a year, I hang a banner outside my storefront. It reads "Thank you to all our customers who helped make this another record year. We love you."

We know this is effective, not because of the favorable response we receive from our fans, but by the attitudes of our competitors.

Proudly displayed inside our dealership (in the restrooms, lobby, and seating area) are eight-by-ten-inch plaques that read, "Let us never forget; our customers made us the championship team we've become."

The Seahawks get it. Should you catch a home game, look for the stadium's flagpole. Flying proudly below the stars and stripes is the home team's blue jersey, number twelve, "The Fans."

REMAIN CONSISTENT

Branding comes from the consistent delivery of a style of service, core message, or product. It's what your customers think of the second they hear your name. A true fan will forgive you if you don't play up to par, but not for long. On the other hand, if you go to McDonald's and order a cheeseburger, but it tastes like one from Burger King, you'll notice the difference immediately. You probably won't be very happy about it.

The brand you sell to your customers determines whether they place their trust and confidence in your company. Imagine your customer telling his friend that you offer an oil change for nineteen dollars, but only when management feels warm and fuzzy. Before long, the abandonment issue will arise—the one your customers inflict on your company when you don't define yourself and remain consistent in delivering your promise.

A surefire way to sustain your brand's pulse is to maintain a constant dialogue with your fan base. If the slightest negative change has begun to emerge, they'll be the first to let you know.

Take Ruby's Hideaway for example. For over six years, Ruby's lobster night produced staggering numbers. Every Thursday night, 400 patrons waited up to two hours to gorge themselves on sweet Australian lobster.

However, in the years that followed, a 30 percent fall-off occurred. The negative numbers alarmed the staff. They knew a competitor had opened across town and offered not only lobster but eight different types of fresh seafood.

"We've been here twenty years and have the home-field advantage. Don't worry," Ruby said.

One night, Ruby sat at the bar with one of her regular customers. "Why haven't I seen you here lately?"

"Truthfully, I enjoy Lorreto's more because over there they treat me like a fan on the fifty-yard line." The customer lowered his drink to his cardboard coaster and leaned practically in Ruby's face. "I tried to tell you guys, but no one listened."

Ouch hard reality for Ruby. Customer comment cards, the Internet, and general word of mouth are great outlets to sniff out how you're perceived and whether you should make adjustments. Once your brand has been established, your survival will depend on maintaining it consistently according to your customers' expectations.

REMEMBERING HIS NAME: GOOD.
REMEMBERING SOMETHING ABOUT HIM: BETTER

She's the redhead who works at UNM Hospital. He's the guy with the hair Steve would love to graft onto the front of his own head. (Really, this guy has just what I'm looking for.) She's the one Juan falls all over when he sees her.

Seriously! Select one thing about each customer and tag her with your personal identification sticker. We interact with thousands of people, and we'd love to sell a vehicle to the majority of them someday. You'll achieve the edge by remembering not only a name, but also where they work, live, and play. Customer relations are relationships.

THERE'S NO RECORD OF A PROBLEM, JUST AN OPPORTUNITY

Joseph, a self-made multimillionaire, purchased the best-made vehicle in the world: a new Rolls Royce. He arranged for the ferry to transport it from its home base in London to France, where he lived. When it arrived, Joseph couldn't wait to drive it home. After a perfect ride of twenty minutes, the Rolls sputtered and died, then it coasted to the edge of the road.

In a frantic fury, Joseph phoned the dealer. They immediately dispatched a team of mechanics to the site. Arriving by company jet, with a transporter waiting, they hit the scene in less that two hours. Once there, they quickly remedied the problem.

Thirty minutes later, Joseph drove away. Week after week, he waited for a bill to arrive. Two months passed. He finally phoned Rolls Royce and asked where his bill was. After all, a team of five technicians had landed a jet and driven twenty miles to fix the problem.

Joseph's call was received by a customer service spokesperson. "Sir, we have no record of a service dispatch to France on that day."

My friends, this is justification. When an internal error

occurs within your organization, take the initiative to fix the problem quickly and efficiently. Do not allow your customers to bear the misfortune of something you can correct. Make sure your team is ready to scramble at any time to fix unexpected errors. You'll discover that very few competitors get this and can achieve it. Instill the mindset, "Problem? What problem?"

TAKE TIME TO LISTEN.
THERE COULD BE A RELATIONSHIP HERE

Andrew came to me referred by a good friend. He was a single dad with a daughter the same age as my granddaughter, Desi. We formed a connection immediately. He needed transportation because his 1987 van was barely running.

My only problem was that he delivered newspapers. That is one profession we as a car dealership can't do business with. The constant stop-and-go acceleration places a severe strain on the transmission and motor. Over time, we've been burned by doing these deals.

I knew Andrew was in dire straits. He kept a grueling schedule: 2:00 a.m. to 5:30 a.m. and 3:00 p.m. to 5:00 p.m. He needed these hours so he could be the one to take his daughter to and from school and day care. He was a hands-on dad who took his role seriously.

I went against policy, took his van in trade, and sold him a car. This deal went down in history as the longest transaction I've ever done. And here's why: I asked him what circumstances had made him a single father.

Andrew looked me straight in the eye. "Her mother over-dosed on heroin in front of the baby. I came home that after-noon to discover that my life had changed without notice."

At that point, I didn't want to stop at selling him a car. My passion for his success instilled in me a desire to help him succeed. Over the next five years, Andrew purchased three vehicles from me, referred his brother and a few friends, has three routes, and is considering starting his own business, contracting out several more.

Andrew's internal problem wasn't fixable; the girl's mom would never return. But like everyone else, he has a story. Take the time to listen. Sometimes a problem is an oppor-tunity to create lasting relationships, both business and personal.

With Andrew's hectic schedule, it would be easy for him to phone in his payment, but on the twenty-third of every month, he and his daughter make the trip to the 5K. I can't help but smile and know this fan would sit in my nosebleed section in any weather to support my team. This is how great fans are created.

THE TAKEAWAY: Here are the five steps to securing the home field advantage:

Step #1: Understand this: the more fans you have, the better the odds of your survival.

Step #2: Establish a brand that keeps these precious assets satisfied.

Step #3: Stay consistent with your brand and deliver it every time, on time.

Step #4: Acknowledge your fans personally. Create lasting relationships with them.

Step #5: Never violate their trust, for their loyalty is your advantage.

CHAPTER 16

THIS IS
YOUR SEASON

DEFENSIVE LINE UP: Should you worry about how much time is left on your play clock? If you don't win the championship this year, there's always next year, right?

OFFENSIVE STRATEGY TAKEN: Emerge victorious by executing your game plan, whether or not it's your season. The good news is that when your season comes, you'll have over fifty time-tested offensive strategies that produce championship results. You can pinpoint your season's arrival by acknowledging and committing to my five truths.

When is your season? In business, it's the time in your life when five issues are reconciled for financial and spiritual growth. This produces confidence in your individual freedom. Supernaturally, you'll rise up and witness overnight success. Amazing opportunities will enter your life with little effort. Believers recognize this awesome state as unmerited favor by grace (Gods Riches At Christ's Expense) received through their faith. This is a natural process that God directs and we obey.

This powerful edge can last several years or be limited to just a few. It terminates as quickly as it begins, leaving few explanations. My desire for you as business owners is that you recognize this brief period and capture everything that will be awarded to you.

Timing is everything, but few recognize this as an opportunity to take action while they are in this sweet spot. The good news is that it usually comes because of something you haven't done versus something you've tried and failed.

⤍

Throughout this book, I've demonstrated the correlation between a successfully managed business and a superbly coached NFL championship team. In football, the battle for supremacy involves days of preparation, the casting of correct personnel, creative leadership, great play calling, and determining whether or not it's your time to win, which is known as your season.

We need the same strategies in order to win in business. However, the seasons differ somewhat between sports and business.

In 2000, I started the $5,000 Car Store. When the inspector pulled up at my place for the first time, he said, "Oh, no, it's another car lot."

At that time, he was right. I struggled to compete in an already-crowded industry. What could go wrong usually did. Every day was a battle for survival in those first five years.

Things began to turn around when I realized that a new season was emerging. I gained a better understanding of five specific truths, and with that understanding came a desire and confidence to obey them.

Five years later, those winning seasons have produced a terrific harvest. Here are five business and spiritual truths that, when recognized, can be gateways to a new season. They all share a common theme, and they exist today as a reminder of the times we live in that only you can change.

THE RIGHT VISION IS ALL IT TAKES
TO CHANGE A STATE OF MIND

On occasion, you might say, "What am I doing? Am I better off going back to work for a company with medical and dental benefits, downsizing from these eighty-hour work weeks, retrofitting those pesky paid vacations back into my schedule? Oh, and I won't have to be the boss anymore. I could coexist with the rank and file and live the rest of my life stress-free."

I battled these emotions, especially when challenging times erupted, sending my stress level through the roof. If you're a believer (this is the key), there will come a time or season when God makes a promise to you. He will fulfill this promise as an assignment with special favor. If you've listened and heard the word, you need to begin preparing immediately. Your season is upon you.

One morning, I was lying in my bed, waiting to greet the new day, wondering which struggles would challenge me that day. Then from out of the blue, God spoke to me: "Get up and prepare, for I'm going to make your company a model for success. I ask only one thing in return. Share these triumphant experiences with others. Do not keep them to yourself."

How would I do this? And then it came to me: "Keep a daily journal and write a playbook so others can prosper too. Share your stories; they'll resonate easily with people who desire success from their businesses."

My friends, this is truly how it happens. God took a semi-successful business run by a simple guy and transformed it into a successful model for others to follow. God can do the same for you. Leave open a window to your receptive mind and allow a vision to enter. I've met many successful people, and their one common denominator is the realization of the importance of acknowledging their visions. When your season arrives, you'll have no time to waver. Make sure your mind is receptive so you can believe it is possible.

SOCIAL SECURITY WON'T BE ENOUGH

I've spent the better part of my adult life attempting to understand the complexities of investing. My conclusion is this: investing in anything you don't fully understand is financial suicide. Perhaps Warren Buffett and James Cramer make it fun, voguish, and simple, but that doesn't mean it's a wise decision for you and me. The current rally that's underway, will disappoint too.

During the largest economic expansion in modern history, the S&P 500 (a snapshot of 500 blue chip companies) is still within a few percentage points of its closing at the end of 1999. How could you have prospered as a self-employed start-up for the last eleven years? Big money circulates in the financial markets. These players belong in a league of their own; it's not a place where we need to participate.

There's no control and very little oversight in this arena. Investing here involves entrusting your money to a company you can read only a few paragraphs about. If you're fortunate, they may allow you to sit in on a conference call.

This doesn't make financial sense to me. Wouldn't it be more prudent to invest your disposable dollars back into your own company's future? After all, this is your business. You control its destiny.

REPUBLICAN OR DEMOCRAT—DOES IT MATTER?

Aren't you tired of politics, about hearing that change is on the way? Next stop: a city near you. Do we need this in our daily lives? Are you counting on them to fix your problems?

When you truly believe that you're the only one who can make the changes that will successfully navigate your vessel, then you're in the right mindset. Your season has begun. Years from now, history will record your ability to succeed. Here's how I envision what my seeds will produce, and, I hope, yours will too.

Someday a family member not yet born will gaze upon your picture and ask, "Who's that?"

You'll be described like this: "This was a person who had the courage to rise up and change her family's directional compass. She received a vision (we know where this originates) and obeyed her heavenly Father's will. Today, because of her courage, this family has evolved into something never before imagined."

This is not a campaign promise, but a historic reality.

IT'S NOT ABOUT THE MONEY

Money is the trophy you receive for winning the game. Don't seek money; seek the victory, its challenges, and the passion it takes to win. Most people misunderstand this concept. When we turn away from calculating profit, from counting every customer as a dollar bill, then we begin to create wealth. Play to win and wealth will come to you in ways you won't believe.

Winning means you invest in others first, because you'll need a complete team (employees, customers, and suppliers) in order to win. When your team finishes first, the trophy you're handed will belong to everyone. The notion that you make money is an illusion. You are granted money because of the fine work you instill into others. You'll prosper with a promotion when you complete this step. I ceased struggling financially when I adopted this strategy.

I'm entrusted to manage millions of dollars during one of the worst economic downturns the world has ever seen.

Anyone who knows me knows I'm happy to invest it back so others can achieve their season. God has allowed me the honorable position of a custodian of his currency, a steward, because he can trust me to do the right thing with it. Wealth creation is not about how much money you have; it's about what you do with it.

SUCCESSFUL OVERTONES WITH A HINT OF STRESS— IT TAKES TIME AND PATIENCE

Napa Valley Cabernet Sauvignon takes about five years to mature into a prize-winning vintage. What makes this nectar spectacular are the trials and tribulations of its growing season. In order to capture the essence of a fine, aged wine, the grapes must first endure what Mother Nature provides. The growing season is nine months, but the season of maturity can be up to five years.

It may seem as if your season will never arrive, and many don't have the patience to wait. I waited five years. The secret is to believe and to anticipate the season he promises. Your roots will never take hold if they're not in fertile ground.

I believe these five observations must be aligned in perfect harmony. This means you must study each one carefully and think about how it applies in your life. Work them through until they become a burning passion you can accept and desire to pursue. You'll know your season has come when you align them one by one into an over-comer's perspective. Go forward and accept victory naturally.

THE TAKEAWAY: Famous last words: Could have—Would have—Should have. Looking back on my successful career with a company I began working for in 1997, I realize that I could have nestled in and stayed there until retirement. They promoted me quickly and promised me a position in the corporation that could have allowed me to implement regional policies.

My employment package included a great salary, bonus program, benefits, travel, power, prestige, and all the perks one could imagine. I could have been completely satisfied, but I wanted to start my own business. (Remember, only few are called.) It could have been a tragedy if I hadn't followed my gifting and pursued my season. There would be no $5,000 Car Store today.

My friends don't fall prey to "I could have." The only thing standing between you and success is not "I could have" but "I didn't—I stayed in my comfort zone."

On Thursday, February 18, I began my morning at the corporate office where I do the majority of my writing. After an hour, I was wrapping things up, heading off to the Manheim Auction, when I received a distress call from my eighty-six-year-old mother. Her obvious pain alerted me that something was terribly wrong. She cried out to me, "I can't see! Everything is blurry, and the pain—it's horrible."

Thursdays are the one day I don't visit with her in the early morning, but we always communicate by phone. Becky happened to call me right then. I told her to contact Mom's caretaker, Julie, who, fortunately for us, lives three minutes away. I told Becky to have Julie get over there stat, since I thought my mom was having a stroke.

I called my mom back. Finally, on the sixth ring, she answered. This time I knew we had to call the paramedics. I stayed on the line with her until Julie arrived. Mom suffered a ruptured aneurism and to this day remains in critical care.

A three-time cancer survivor (without chemotherapy), my mother is one tough woman. A couple of days after the aneurism, she struck up a conversation with me which would have a major impact on how I finish the *Playbook's* last segment.

With her confidence badly shaken, she began to reminisce about her working days. Whispering from beneath her oxygen mask, she told me why she never started her own business. (This is something we'd never discussed before.)

"I would have, but rearing you and your sister was more important. That's the problem with today's kids, there's no one watching them. [She's right.]

"Maybe I would have thought about it more after you kids were raised; after all, I was sitting in the catbird seat just before the big California coastal real estate boom. While I worked as an assistant to the owners of Sea Cottage Real Estate [David and Cathy, the good friends of Colonel Scobie], they gave me several opportunities to invest with them. Was that God speaking to my heart? I would have, but by then I was fifty-eight and didn't want to take the risk.

"Lying here, not knowing how many days I have left,

looking back, knowing what I know now, I realize I would have never passed up any opportunity God offered if I'd known things would have turned out like this."

⌒

Are you wondering whether it's the right time to branch out and start a small business or dramatically improve an existing one?

I started my first business, the Culinarian Catering Company, when I was nineteen. One night after a pre-wedding dinner party for thirty guests, I walked upstairs to the lounge. Sitting at the end of the bar with our commodore and his girlfriend was a man I'd seen before but couldn't place.

I nudged the bartender. "Who is that sitting next to Al and Carol?"

He whispered, "Don't you recognize him? That's Gary Dahl, the guy who invented the Pet Rock. Steve, you've served him lunch a few times."

I could never resist an opportunity to talk to a marketing genius. The "Rock" had a short stint at super success. In 1975, Gary and some friends were having some drinks and joking about their pets and the trials and tribulations involved in keeping them. Gary amused his companions with the idea of the ultimate effortless pet, complete with instructions and accessories.

A few months later, the craze had swept the country. The first question asked at a party in those days was, "What's your rock's name?"

Before the Pet Rock phenomenon, Gary ran a marketing company in Los Gatos, California, patiently awaiting his season. He periodically docked his sailboat at the Metropolitan Yacht Club, where he was an honorary member.

I asked him, "What's your advice for someone starting out in business?"

His response was short and stern. "Don't ever let your life go by saying, 'I should have.'"

That was great advice, Gary, and I've never forgotten it. In

> *"Don't ever let your life go by saying, 'I should have.'"*

fact, listening to you that night inspired me to begin looking for a buyer for my catering business so I could pursue other business interests. Six months later, I sold the Culinarian for a huge profit. Gary sold over five million rocks in six months and became one of the greatest marketers of the twentieth century.

Too many people choose the wait-and-see approach. They're content sitting on the bench, hoping the coach doesn't motion for their participation. Don't lose out on the one opportunity to realize your winning season.

Thank you for allowing me to share with you these past few hours. I believe your purchase of *The Playbook for Small Businesses* will make a difference in your business. You are now a registered member of Business Boost of North America. As a valued guest, you're invited to attend one of our annual celebrations. Keep this copy as your free admission. See you there!

About the Author

Steve Henry started the Culinarian Catering Company at age nineteen and sold it two years later at a staggering profit. The Culinarian was the first of his six businesses throughout his thirty-year career as an entrepreneur.

In 2000, he founded the $5,000 Car Store, a car dealership and finance company. He sold over five hundred vehicles last year. With the expansion of his business model and the opening of his third store, revenues will surpass four million dollars this year. He forecasts operating ten stores in three states before the end of 2012.

Steve, his wife, Becky, and granddaughter, Desiree, live in northern Rio Rancho, New Mexico, which is nestled among the breathtaking Sandia Mountains.

LaVergne, TN USA
30 June 2010
187951LV00003B/80/P